Patrick Crowley

Enlightened Christmas

1979

D1336742

THE COLLECTED WORKS OF ALDOUS HUXLEY

★

*TEXTS AND PRETEXTS*

## By ALDOUS HUXLEY

★

THE LETTERS OF ALDOUS HUXLEY

### Novels

CROME YELLOW
ANTIC HAY
THOSE BARREN LEAVES
POINT COUNTER POINT
BRAVE NEW WORLD
EYELESS IN GAZA
AFTER MANY A SUMMER
TIME MUST HAVE A STOP
APE AND ESSENCE
THE GENIUS AND THE GODDESS
ISLAND

### Short Stories

LIMBO • MORTAL COILS
LITTLE MEXICAN
TWO OR THREE GRACES
BRIEF CANDLES
COLLECTED SHORT STORIES

### Biography

GREY EMINENCE
THE DEVILS OF LOUDUN

### Essays and Belles Lettres

ON THE MARGIN
ALONG THE ROAD
PROPER STUDIES
DO WHAT YOU WILL
MUSIC AT NIGHT &
VULGARITY IN LITERATURE
TEXTS AND PRETEXTS (Anthology)
THE OLIVE TREE
ENDS AND MEANS (An Enquiry
into the Nature of Ideals)
THE ART OF SEEING
THEMES AND VARIATIONS
THE PERENNIAL PHILOSOPHY
SCIENCE, LIBERTY AND PEACE
THE DOORS OF PERCEPTION
HEAVEN AND HELL
ADONIS AND THE ALPHABET
BRAVE NEW WORLD REVISITED
COLLECTED ESSAYS
LITERATURE AND SCIENCE

### Travel

JESTING PILATE
BEYOND THE MEXIQUE BAY
BEYOND THE MEXIQUE BAY (Illustrated)

### Poetry and Drama

VERSES AND A COMEDY
(including early poems, Leda, The Cicadas
and The World of Light, a Comedy)
THE GIOCONDA SMILE

### For Children

THE CROWS OF PEARBLOSSOM

# TEXTS
# AND PRETEXTS

## AN ANTHOLOGY
## WITH COMMENTARIES

*By*

ALDOUS HUXLEY

1974

CHATTO & WINDUS
LONDON

PUBLISHED BY

Chatto & Windus

LONDON

★

Clarke, Irwin & Co. Ltd.

TORONTO

ISBN 0 7011 0816 9

*First published in 1932*
*First issued in a Collected Edition 1949*
*First issued in this edition 1973*

Introduction and Commentaries
© Mrs. Laura Huxley 1932

Printed in Great Britain by
Redwood Press Limited
Trowbridge, Wiltshire

# CONTENTS

# CONTENTS

Grateful acknowledgments are due to the following for permission to print certain copyright material : the poet's family and the Oxford University Press for the quotations from *Gerard Manley Hopkins* ; Messrs. Ingpen *&* Grant for those from *Edward Thomas* ; Mr. Derek Patmore for certain pieces from *Coventry Patmore* ; Messrs. Elkin Mathews *&* Marrot for the poem by *Lionel Johnson* ; *M. Paul Valéry* and the Éditions de la Nouvelle Revue Française for the poem by himself, entitled ' Les Pas,' from his volume ' Poésies ' ; the executors of *Stéphane Mallarmé* and the Éditions de la Nouvelle Revue Française for the poems by Mallarmé, from the collected edition ' Poésies ' ; and the Mercure de France for the poems by *Rimbaud*.

# INTRODUCTION

An anthology compiled in mid-slump ? Fiddling, you protest indignantly, while Rome burns. But perhaps Rome would not now be burning if the Romans had taken a more intelligent interest in their fiddlers.

We tend to think and feel in terms of the art we like ; and if the art we like is bad, then our thinking and feeling will be bad. And if the thinking and feeling of most of the individuals composing a society is bad, is not that society in danger ? To sit on committees and discuss the gold standard are doubtless public-spirited actions. But not the only public-spirited actions. They also serve who only bother their heads about art.

Just as the uncivilized try to copy the civilized—even when the civilized are quite unworthy of imitation— so does life try to copy art—even when it is bad. Hence the importance of good art.

> Quando leggemmo il disiato riso
> esser baciato da cotanto amante,
> questi, che mai da me non fia diviso,
>
> la bocca mi baciò tutto tremante :
> Galeotto fu il libro, e chi lo scrisse ;
> quel giorno più non vi leggemmo avante.

' The pandar was the book and he who wrote it.' Knowing the power of art to mould life in its own image, many puritans have wished to abolish art altogether. If they had confined their iconoclasm to bad art, there might have been some sense in them. Boys and girls who have Dante for their pandar are more likely to make love with style, handsomely, than those whose spiritual food is drawn from the magazines and the films.

I read, not long ago, the report of a discourse pronounced by an eminent American clergyman on the Popular Song. The sermon was a panegyric. Popular songs, according to this reverend gentleman, are repositories of wisdom and sound moral doctrine. A man has only to mark, learn and inwardly digest the successes of each season (at any rate, those which are not specifically erotic) to know his whole duty. Skies of blue, hearts so true, You-ou—jazz will provide him with the most cheering of philosophies, the purest of ethics. If he lives what the negroes bawl through the noise of the saxophones, he will live well. In a word, an education in popular songs is the modern equivalent of an education in the humanities.

Blessed, we are told, are the poor in spirit.

Jazz lyrics—the spiritual food of the masses. But even the educated few are not much better provided. Science advances from discovery to discovery, political and economic changes follow one another with a bewildering rapidity. The educated have to ' keep up.' They are so busy keeping up that they seldom have time to read any author who thinks and feels and writes with style. In a rapidly changing age, there is a real danger that being well informed may prove incompatible with being cultivated. To be well informed, one must read quickly a great number of merely instructive books. To be cultivated, one must read slowly and with a lingering appreciation the comparatively few books that have been written by men who lived, thought and felt with style.

As the influence of religion declines, the social importance of art increases. We must beware of exchanging good religion for bad art.

In the course of the last half century, the conceptions in terms of which men interpret their experience have been altered by science out of all recognition. Superficially, therefore, much of the great poetry of the past is out of date. But only superficially; for the fundamental experience remains almost unaltered. It is not difficult to decode, as it were, the older interpretations, to translate them into our terms. This is one of the things I have tried to do in my commentaries.

It would have been better, obviously, to write it all oneself, poetical text as well as commentary—if any commentary were needed, that is to say; for a contemporary text would require no translation into modern terms, no decoding from one system of philosophy into another. It would have been better, I repeat, to write it all oneself—a new Divine Comedy;

and, if I had the abilities of Dante, I should certainly undertake the task. But, in company with all but about half a dozen of the men and women who have lived in the last thousand years, I lack these abilities. So I must content myself with picking up these broken and half-forgotten fragments from the past and fitting them, one here, another there, into their appropriate places in the jumbled mosaic of contemporary experience.

Would even Dante's abilities suffice to inform our vast and·swiftly changing chaos, to build it up into a harmonious composition, to impose a style ? One may venture to doubt it. There is too much raw material, of too many kinds ; and some of the kinds (as, for example, the experience of the urban industrial or clerical worker) seem almost too hopelessly mechanical ever to be given style. And yet it is only by poets that the life of any epoch can be synthesized. Encyclopaedias and guides to knowledge cannot do it, for the good reason that they affect only the intellectual surface of a man's life. The lower layers, the core of his being, they leave untouched.

The Ideal Man of the eighteenth century was the Rationalist ; of the seventeenth, the Christian Stoic ; of the Renaissance, the Free Individual ; of the Middle Ages, the Contemplative Saint. And what is our Ideal Man ? On what grand and luminous mythological figure does contemporary humanity attempt to model itself ? The question is embarrassing. Nobody knows. And, in spite of all the laudable efforts of the Institute for Intellectual Co-operation to fabricate an acceptable Ideal Man for the use of Ministers of Education, nobody, I suspect, will know until such time as a major poet appears upon the scene with the unmistakable revelation. Meanwhile, one must be content to go on piping up for reason and realism and a certain decency.

The poet is, etymologically, the maker. Like all makers, he requires a stock of raw materials—in his case, experience. Now experience is not a matter of having actually swum the Hellespont, or danced with the dervishes, or slept in a doss-house. It is a matter of sensibility and intuition, of seeing and hearing the significant things, of paying attention at the right moments, of understanding and co-ordinating. Experience is not what happens to a man ; it is what a man does with what happens to him. It is a gift for dealing with the accidents of existence, not the accidents themselves. By a happy dispensation of nature, the poet generally possesses the gift of experience in conjunction with that of expression. What he says so well is therefore intrinsically of value.

Sometimes the gift of saying exists alone, in strange divorce from the gift of seeing and understanding. There is D'Annunzio's thunderous eloquence about next to nothing ; there are Swinburne's melodious variations on all but non-existent themes. But, generally, saying and seeing go together. The people who have understood most have been endowed with the gift of telling what they understood. I doubt if there have been many Miltons who remained mute and inglorious.


Listening to the poet,
>    . . . the nightingale thought, ' I have sung many songs,
>  But never a one so gay ;
> For he sings of what the world will be,
>    When the years have died away.'

Personally, I must confess, I am more interested in what the world is now than in what it will be, or what it might be, if improbable conditions were fulfilled.


Poetry ' was ever thought to have some participation of divineness, because it doth raise and erect the mind by submitting the shows of things to the desires of the mind ; whereas reason doth buckle and bow the mind unto the nature of things.' This means, in modern jargon, that poetry is admirable only when it deals in wish-fulfilments. With this judgment I profoundly disagree. And, fortunately, many excellent poets have shown, by their practice, that they do too. There is, in every language, a huge mass of wish-fulfilment poetry ; but there is also a great deal of poetry that renders, or that passes judgment on, man's actual experience—a great deal of poetry, in a word, that ' doth buckle and bow the mind to the nature of things.' For me, such poetry is by far the most interesting and valuable.

> So every spirit, as it is most pure,
> And hath in it the more of heavenly light,
> So it the fairer body doth procure
> To habit in, and is more fairly dight
> With cheerful grace and amiable sight :
> For of the soul the body form doth take ;
> And soul is form, and doth the body make.

This submits ' the shows of things to the desires of the mind ' with a vengeance ! But does it thereby ' raise and erect the mind ' ? Not mine, at any rate. I have always thought it rather degrading for an adult to believe in fairy stories.

I prefer being sober to even the rosiest and most agreeable intoxications. The peyotl-trances of Swinburne, for example, have always left me perfectly *compos mentis* ; I do not catch the infection. Much even of Shelley's poetry is, for me, too swimmingly the coloured dream ; and even when it is not dreamlike, its long-drawn imprecision is apt to flow past me, unmovingly. Shelley's effects, like Spenser's, are mainly cumulative, and I lack the patience to let them accumulate. I like things to be said with precision and as concisely as possible. This does not mean, of course, that I would like all poets to say their say in four-line epigrams and the style of Voltaire. Certain things can only be expressed at considerable length and in

7

terms of the most improbable metaphors, an abracadabra of magic syllables. There are occasions when the poet who would write precisely must be (by the standards of text-book prose) obscure and fantastic.

Most poets have been aware of the greatness of the poetic function, have respected in themselves that touch of divinity which made the Romans call poet and prophet by the same name. But many of them seem to have confused poetry with verse—to have thought that there was something meritorious in the mere act of writing in metre, some quality of sacredness in a metrical composition. The result was that they published, as poetry, stuff no more significant than so much literary chit-chat in a Sunday paper.

' Should the Modern Girl wear Underclothes ? A Thoughtful Article specially contributed to the *Sabbath Express* by the Poet Laureate.' One can visualize the headlines boldly sprawling across page eleven. Wordsworth would have been paid, handsomely, for such outpourings ; and his indiscretions would have been forgotten before the week was out. But he preferred to write things like ' The Power of Sound '—to write them and, what was much worse, to publish them in his Poetical Works. We are put to the endless trouble of sifting this worthless rubbish in search of gems, which generally prove to be non-existent.

> Why need I say, Louisa dear,
> How glad I am to see you here,
>   A lovely convalescent ;

> Risen from the bed of pain and fear
> And feverish heat incessant.

Such stuff, alas, is more characteristic of Coleridge's muse than *Kubla Khan*. Shelley, too, is often as featureless and chaotic as the Blake of the Prophetic Books.

> Obedient to the sweep of aery song,
>    The mighty ministers
> Unfurled their prismy wings.
>    The magic car moved on ;
> The night was fair, innumerable stars
>    Studded heaven's dark blue vault ;
>    The eastern wave grew pale
>    With the first smile of morn. . . .

And so on, indefinitely. It is mere automatic writing ; almost any medium could do as well. As for Wordsworth, he had not even the excuse of automatism.

> The turbaned Race are poured in thickening swarms
> Along the West ; though driven from Aquitaine,
> The Crescent glitters on the towers of Spain,
> And soft Italia feels renewed alarms ;
> The scimitar, that yields not to the charms
> Of ease, the narrow Bosphorus will disdain ;
> Nor long (that crossed) would Grecian hills detain
> Their tents, and check the current of their arms.
> Then blame not those who, by the mightiest lever
> Known to the moral world, Imagination,
> Upheave, so seems it, from her natural station
> All Christendom—they sweep along (was never
> So huge a host !)—to tear from the Unbeliever
> The precious Tomb, their haven of salvation.

Lines like these—and there are thousands of them in

Wordsworth's various volumes—can only have been written in the fullest consciousness, laboriously. The thought is exceedingly depressing.

That good poets should sometimes, or even generally, write badly is not, after all, very surprising. Auspicious circumstances must conspire with exceptional gifts ; the mind must be seconded by its incalculable companion of flesh and blood, not crossed and hindered. The surprising thing, I repeat, is not that good poets should sometimes write badly ; it is, rather, that they should publish these unfortunate essays ; that they should not have been self-critical enough to consign them to their proper place, the waste-paper basket.

The early anthologists were in a position to reject only the bad. The last must also throw away much that is admirable. The well-known excellences are so familiar, so easily accessible, that it seems hardly worth while to reprint them yet once more. Luckily, however, there are more fish in the sea of literature than ever came out of it—at any rate, in the nets of Palgrave and Quiller-Couch and Bridges.

# VISITATIONS

Who would have thought my shrivelled heart
Could have recovered greenness ?   It was gone
Quite under ground : as flowers depart
To see their mother root, when they have blown,
    Where they together,
    All the hard weather,
Dead to the world, keep house unknown.

These are thy wonders, Lord of Power,
Killing and quickening, bringing down to hell
And up to heaven in an hour ;
Making a chiming of a passing bell.
    We said amiss
    This or that is :
Thy word is all, if we could spell. . . .

And now in age I bud again
After so many deaths I live and write ;
I once more smell the dew and rain
And relish versing ; O my only Light !
    It cannot be
    That I am he
On whom thy tempests fell all night.
GEORGE HERBERT.

How rich, O Lord, how fresh thy visits are !
'Twas but just now my bleak leaves hopeless hung
    Sullied with dust and mud ;
Each snarling blast shot through me, and did share
Their youth and beauty ; cold showers nipped and
    wrung
    Their spiciness and blood.

But since thou didst in one sweet glance survey
Their sad decays, I flourish and once more
    Breathe all perfumes and spice ;
I smell a dew like myrrh and all the day
Wear in my bosom a full sun ; such store
    Hath one beam from thy eyes.
But, ah, my God, what fruit hast thou of this ?
What one poor leaf did ever I let fall
    To wait upon thy wreath ?
Thus thou all day a thankless weed dost dress,
And when thou hast done, a stench or fog is all
    The odour I bequeath.

HENRY VAUGHAN.

The climate of the mind is positively English in its variableness and instability. Frost, sunshine, hopeless drought and refreshing rains succeed one another with bewildering rapidity. Herbert is the poet of this inner weather. Accurately, in a score of lyrics unexcelled for flawless purity of diction and appositeness of imagery, he has described its changes and interpreted, in terms of a mystical philosophy, their significance. Within his limits he achieves a real perfection.

Vaughan treats the same theme, but less perfectly. Lacking Herbert's artistic ability and artistic conscience, he occasionally (in this as in his other poems) ' lets one down,' as Herbert hardly ever does. By way of compensation, however, he also occasionally ' lets one up ' to heights which Herbert as seldom reaches. Most great poets let their readers down much more often than they let them up, and to abysses almost as deep as their peaks are high. Why does Shakespeare

12

stand so manifestly in a class apart ? Because he lets us
up higher and far more frequently, down incomparably
less often and less low, than any other poet.

J'ai vu parfois, au fond d'un théâtre banal
    Qu'enflammait l'orchestre sonore,
Une fée allumer dans un ciel infernal
    Une miraculeuse aurore ;
J'ai vu parfois au fond d'un théâtre banal

Un être qui n'était que lumière, or et gaze,
    Terrasser l'énorme Satan ;
Mais mon cœur, que jamais ne visite l'extase,
    Est un théâtre où l'on attend
Toujours, toujours en vain, l'Être aux ailes de gaze !

               CHARLES BAUDELAIRE.

Dear night ! this world's defeat ;
The stop to busy fools ; care's check and curb ;
The day of spirits ; my soul's calm retreat,
Which none disturb !
Christ's progress and his prayer time ;
The hours to which high Heaven doth chime ;

God's silent searching flight ;
When my Lord's head is filled with dew, and all
His locks are wet with the clear drops of night ;
His still, soft call ;
His knocking time ; the soul's dumb watch,
When spirits their fair kindred catch.

Were all my loud evil days
Calm and unhaunted as is thy dark tent,
Whose peace but by some angel's wing or voice
Is seldom rent ;

Then I in Heaven all the long year
Would keep, and never wander here.
But living where the sun
Doth all things wake, and where all mix and tire
Themselves and others, I consent and run
To every mire,
And by this world's ill-guiding light,
Err more than I can do by night.

There is in God (some say)
A deep, but dazzling darkness ; as men here
Say it is late and dusky, because they
See not all clear ;
O for that night ! where I in him
Might live invisible and dim.

HENRY VAUGHAN.

Tes pas, enfants de mon silence,
Saintement, lentement placés,
Vers le lit de ma vigilance
Procèdent, muets et glacés.

Personne pure, ombre divine,
Qu'ils sont doux, tes pas retenus !
Dieux ! . . . tous les dons que je devine
Viennent à moi sur ces pieds nus !

Si, de tes lèvres avancées,
Tu prépares, pour l'apaiser,
A l'habitant de mes pensées
La nourriture d'un baiser,

Ne hâte pas cet acte tendre,
Douceur d'être et de n'être pas,
Car j'ai vécu de vous attendre,
Et mon cœur n'était que vos pas.

PAUL VALÉRY.

It happens occasionally that 'spirits their fair kindred catch'; or rather, to use a more guarded philosophical language, that they catch themselves —make themselves manifest by circumventing or temporarily abolishing the psychological obstacles which normally prevent us from becoming blissfully conscious of our solidarity with the universe.

For most of us, our everyday, daytime existence consists of an unbroken series of such obstacles. It is only exceptionally, when we are free from distractions, in the silence and darkness of the night, or of night's psychological equivalent, that we become aware of our own souls and, along with them, of what seems the soul of the world. In the two poems I have quoted, Vaughan describes the auspicious circumstances, Valéry the oncoming of the inenarrably beautiful event which they render possible.

How should I praise thee, Lord, how should my
    rhymes
Gladly engrave thy love in steel,
If what my soul doth feel sometimes,
My soul might ever feel !

Although there were some forty heavens or more,
Sometimes I peer above them all ;
Sometimes I hardly reach a score,
Sometimes to hell I fall.
                GEORGE HERBERT.

But first a hush of peace—a soundless calm descends ;
The struggle of distress and fierce impatience ends.

Mute music soothes my breast—unuttered harmony
That I could never dream, till Earth was lost to me.

Then dawns the Invisible : the Unseen its truth
    reveals ;
My outward sense is gone, my inward essence feels ;
Its wings are almost free—its home, its harbour
    found,
Measuring the gulf, it stoops, and dares the final
    bound.

O dreadful is the check—intense the agony—
When the ear begins to hear, and the eye begins to
    see ;
When the pulse begins to throb—the brain to think
    again—
The soul to feel the flesh, and the flesh to feel the
    chain.

EMILY BRONTË.

If, if, if. . . . How many conditional clauses there
are in the writings of the mystics !

> How should I praise thee, Lord, . . .
> If what my soul doth feel sometimes,
> My soul might ever feel ;

>               might mortal breath
> Express the passion then inspired,
> Evil would die a natural death,
> And nothing transient be desired ;

Could we but live at will upon this perfect height,
Could we but always keep the passion of this peace . . .
Then were we all divine.

But the soul *cannot* always feel what it feels some-times ; mortal breath *cannot* express the passion then inspired ; and the perfect height *cannot* be lived on, only visited. The clauses remain conditional—always. If they were fulfilled, man would lose all the qualities which we admire as distinctively human. Virtue is possible only in an unethical universe and in beings whose minds are so made that they cannot always remain at their highest pitch. Consistently rewarded, virtue would cease to be virtue ; and if the soul did not have its long weary spells of feeling the flesh and the flesh of feeling the chain, there would be no such things as heroism and endurance. Man might be happier if the conditional clauses of the mystics were fulfilled—happier, but less interesting and, at bottom, ignobler.

Earth trembled from her entrails, as again
In pangs, and Nature gave a second groan ;
Sky loured and, muttering thunder, some sad drops
Wept at completing of the mortal sin
Original ; while Adam took no thought,
Eating his fill, nor Eve to iterate
Her former trespass feared, the more to soothe
Him with her loved society ; that now,
As with new wine intoxicated both,
They swim in mirth, and fancy that they feel
Divinity within them breeding wings
Wherewith to scorn the Earth. But that false fruit
Far other operation first displayed,
Carnal desire inflaming.

JOHN MILTON.

Milton is almost always meticulously precise in his language. Which makes his present lapse the more surprising. For nobody can fancy that he feels something. We either do feel or don't. Occasions arise when, by a process of inference after the fact, we decide that what we had supposed, at the time, to be the cause of the feeling was not the cause, or that its significance was not in fact what we had imagined. In these circumstances we can say that we felt what we fancied to be a feeling of such and such a nature. But to say that we fancied that we felt this feeling is quite unjustifiable. The feeling is a fact of immediate experience—given and unalterable. Fancy can affect only our subsequent attempts at explanation and interpretation.

By the Catholic Church ecstatic feelings are regarded as being intrinsically neither good nor bad. It is by their subsequent fruits—the moral fruits which they bear when the mystic has returned to common life—that they are judged. If the fruits are bad, then (such is the judgment of the Church) the ecstasy was sent by the Devil; if good, it came from God. There is nothing in the feeling itself to indicate its source. In practice, the ecclesiastical authorities are always extremely cautious and sceptical in their handling of ecstatics. They do not pronounce themselves until there has been plenty of time for the moral fruits of the experience to ripen.

As a practical policy this is excellent; indeed, it is the only policy that an organized Church could possibly pursue. Ecstatic states may be valuable in themselves ; but they are very rare. Life must be lived in the main on another, unecstatic plane. The man who has one hour of ecstasy in every hundred and lives badly for the remaining ninety-nine hours cannot expect to receive a testimonial of sanctity for what he does, or is, or learns in the hour when, by definition he is ' not himself.'

Practically, I repeat, this is excellent. But theoretically it is not quite so satisfactory. The theory of ecstasy is that it is a state of union with a higher being ; that it provides knowledge not merely of something in the mind, but of something in the universe at large, something which cannot be known (except by remote and uncertain inference) in any other way. If this is so and if, as experience seems to show, there is no intrinsic difference between one ecstatic feeling and another, then all ecstasies should be regarded as valuable, irrespective of their causes and their subsequent results. The eating of ' the false fruit ' caused Adam and Eve to feel (really and actually) ' divinity within them breeding wings wherewith to scorn the Earth.' The fact that it then ' far other operation first displayed, carnal desire inflaming ' is quite irrelevant. In itself, one ecstasy is as good as another. It does not matter how the ecstasy is produced—whether by oncoming epilepsy, as in the case of Dostoevsky's Idiot, by voluntarily holding the breath and squinting at the tip of the nose, as with the Indians, by drinking wine, like the Persian dervishes, by fasting and self-hypnotism, the methods of the more refined ecstatics, or finally by mere accident, by a happy conjunction of physiological and mental circumstances. What it produces—whether good works or carnal desire, poetry or a crapula—is equally indifferent. While it lasts it is felt to be a supernatural state ; it provides us with otherwise inaccessible knowledge about ourselves and, according to the theory, about the world.

# COUNTRY ECSTASIES

*(Whitman had two studies where he read : one was the top of an omnibus, and the other a small mass of sand, entirely uninhabited, far out in the ocean, called Coney Island.—* M. D. CONWAY, 1866.)

### The Revelation

An idle poet, here and there,
  Looks round him, but, for all the rest,
The world, unfathomably fair,
  Is duller than a witling's jest.

Love wakes men, once a lifetime each ;
  They lift their heavy lids and look ;
And, lo, what one sweet page can teach
  They read with joy, then shut the book.

And some give thanks, and some blaspheme,
  And most forget ; but either way,
That, and the child's unheeded dream,
  Is all the light of all their day.

COVENTRY PATMORE.

The outcry against the Impressionists proved that the great mass of human beings not only find the external world ' duller than a witling's jest,' but are normally incapable of seeing it. With unprecedented accuracy the Impressionists. painted what they actually saw. They put their visual impressions straight on to the canvas and left them there—raw, so to speak, and mentally undigested. People were outraged. It was only natural. They were not used to seeing the shapes

21

and colours revealed by their sensations. Their minds generalized the brute facts and interpreted them ; what they were used to seeing was what almost all of us ordinarily see—visualized words, the Platonic ideas of Tree, Cloud and so forth. The actual, particular tree or cloud seemed impossibly queer, when the Impressionists revealed it to them ; they were furious. Custom, for us, has staled the Impressionists. We look at their pictures and no longer feel that we are being made fools of and insulted. Sometimes, by luck or (trained by them) with a deliberate effort, we are able to see the external world with their innocent and unbiassed eyes . . . see it for a little *sub specie momenti*. But, strangely and mysteriously, *sub specie momenti* is somehow *sub specie aeternitatis*. Our immediate impressions of actuality, on the rare occasions when we contrive to see with the eyes of children or convalescents, of artists or lovers, seem to have a quality of supernaturalness. What we ordinarily call ' nature ' and find duller than a witling's jest is in fact the system of generalizations and utilitarian symbols which we construct from our sensations. Sometimes, however, we are made directly and immediately aware of our sensations ; it is an apocalypse ; they seem supernatural. But it is through sensations that we come into contact with the external world, the world of Nature with a capital N. Hence a seeming paradox : external Nature is supernatural ; and the supernatural, because mental, universe in which we do our daily living is all too natural—natural to the point of dullness.

22

Look at the stars ! look, look up at the skies !
O look at all the fire-folk sitting in the air !
The bright boroughs, the circle-citadels there !
Down in dim woods the diamond delves ! the elves'-
    eyes !
The grey lawns cold where gold, where quickgold lies !
Wind-beat whitebeam ! airy abeles set on a flare !
Flake-doves sent floating forth at a farmyard scare !—
Ah well ! It is all a purchase, all is a prize.

Buy then ! bid then !—What ?—Prayer, patience,
    alms, vows.
Look, look : a May-mess, like on orchard boughs !
Look ! March-bloom, like on mealed-with-yellow
    sallows !
These are indeed the barn ; withindoors house
The shocks. This piece-bright paling shuts the spouse
Christ home, Christ and his mother and all the
    hallows.

GERARD MANLEY HOPKINS.

The unthrift sun shot vital gold,
    A thousand pieces,
And heaven its azure did unfold,
    Chequered with snowy fleeces.
    The air was all in spice.
        And every bush
A garland wore : thus fed my eye,
    But all the ear lay hush.

Only a little fountain lent
    Some use for ears,
And on the dumb shades language spent,
    The music of her tears.

HENRY VAUGHAN.

Glory be to God for dappled things—
For skies of couple-colour as a brinded cow ;
For rose-moles all in stipple upon trout that swim ;
Fresh-firecoal chestnut-falls ; finches' wings ;
Landscape plotted and pieced—fold, fallow and
    plough ;
And all trades, their gear and tackle and trim.

All things counter, original, spare, strange ;
Whatever is fickle, freckled (who knows how ?)
With swift, slow ; sweet, sour ; adazzle, dim ;
He fathers-forth, whose beauty is past change :
    Praise him.      GERARD MANLEY HOPKINS.

This sycamore, oft musical with bees—
Such tents the Patriarchs loved.  O long unharmed
May all its agèd boughs o'er-canopy
The small round basin, which this jutting stone
Keeps pure from falling leaves !  Long may the Spring,
Quietly as a sleeping infant's breath,
Send up cold waters to the traveller
With soft and even pulse !  Nor ever cease
Yon tiny cone of sand its soundless dance,
Which, at the bottom, like a Fairy's page,
As merry and no taller, dances still,
Nor wrinkles the smooth surface of the fount.
Here twilight is and coolness ; here is moss,
A soft seat, and a deep and ample shade.
Thou may'st toil far and find no second tree.
Drink, Pilgrim, here ; here rest !  And if thy heart
Be innocent, here too shalt thou refresh
Thy spirit, listening to some gentle sound,
Or passing gale, or hum of murmuring bees.
      SAMUEL TAYLOR COLERIDGE.

COUNTRY ECSTASIES

The world is charged with the grandeur of God.
  It will flame out, like shining from shook foil ;
  It gathers to a greatness, like the ooze of oil
Crushed.  Why do men then now not reck his rod ?
Generations have trod, have trod, have trod ;
  And all is seared with trade ;  bleared, smeared
      with toil ;
  And wears man's smudge and shares man's smell :
      the soil
Is bare now, nor can foot feel, being shod.

And for all this, nature is never spent ;
  There lives the dearest freshness deep down things ;
And though the last lights off the black West went
  Oh, morning, at the brown brink eastward,
      springs—
Because the Holy Ghost over the bent
  World broods with warm breast and with ah !
      bright wings.

GERARD MANLEY HOPKINS.

The very name of God

Sounds like a juggler's charm ; and, bold with joy,
(Portentous sight !) the owlet Atheism,
Sailing on obscene wings athwart the noon,
Drops his blue-fringèd lids and holds them close,
And hooting at the glorious sun in Heaven,
Cries out, ' Where is it ? '

SAMUEL TAYLOR COLERIDGE.

Thus I, easy philosopher,
Among the birds and trees confer,
And little now to make me wants
Or of the fowls, or of the plants . . .

Already I begin to call
In their most learned original ;
And where I language want, my signs
The bird upon the bough divines,
And more attentive there doth sit
Than if she were with lime-twigs knit.
No leaf does tremble in the wind
Which I, returning, cannot find.
Out of these scattered Sibyl's leaves
Strange prophecies my phancy weaves ;
And in one history consumes,
Like Mexique paintings, all. the plumes,
What Rome, Greece, Palestine e'er said.
I in this light mosaic read.
Thrice happy he who, not mistook,
Hath read in Nature's mystic book.

ANDREW MARVELL.

It seems I have no tears left.  They should have
    fallen—
Their ghosts, if tears have ghosts, did fall—that day
When twenty hounds streamed by me, not yet
    combed out
But still all equals in their rage of gladness
Upon the scent, made one, like a great dragon
In Blooming Meadow that bends towards the sun
And once bore hops :  and on that other day,
When I stepped out from the double-shadowed
    Tower
Into an April morning, stirring and sweet
And warm.  Strange solitude was there, and silence.
A mightier charm than any in the Tower
Possessed the courtyard.  They were changing guard,
Soldiers in line, young English countrymen,

26

Fair-haired and ruddy, in white tunics.  Drums
And fifes were playing ' The British Grenadiers.'
The men, the music piercing that solitude
And silence, told me truths I had not dreamed,
And have forgotten since that beauty passed.

                                   EDWARD THOMAS.

For those who have actually *felt* the supernatural
quality of nature  dogmatic atheism seems absurd.
But Marvell is right : it is easy to make mistakes when
one is reading ' Nature's mystic book.'  It is easy, as
Thomas implies, to rationalize, quite arbitrarily, in
terms of some ready-made philosophy, feelings which,
in themselves, are dim and indescribable.  (Thomas's
strict honesty is rare ; few poets have been content to
set down baldly what they felt without at the same
time expounding or implying some cosmic theory to
explain why they felt it.  Thus, Hopkins is moved by
the spectacle of the stars and accounts for his emotion
by the hypothesis that ' this piece-bright paling shuts
the spouse Christ home.')

What most ' nature poets' are apt to forget is that the
immediately apprehended quality of things is not
invariably a quality of supernatural beauty ; it is
also, on occasions, a quality of supernatural evil,
supernatural ugliness.  And even the loveliness is
sometimes supernaturally remote and uncaring.  The
owlet atheism shuts his eyes not only to the glorious sun
in heaven, but also to the dark malignities of jungle
and swamp and arctic desert.  He is unaware of the
heavenly loveliness of flowers or a landscape ; but he
is also unaware of the hellishly ironic irrelevance of

                                                    27

their loveliness. Hardy's eyes were wide open to this aspect of the world ; Baudelaire's too.

> Quelquefois dans un beau jardin,
>     Où je trainais mon atonie,
> J'ai senti comme une ironie
>     Le soleil déchirer mon sein ;
>
> Et le printemps et la verdure
>     Ont tant humilié mon cœur,
> Que j'ai puni sur une fleur
>     L'insolence de la nature.

Baudelaire would have been very much happier if he could have dropped his lids and held them close against the sun.

> Beneath is spread, like a green sea,
> The waveless plain of Lombardy,
> Bounded by the vaporous air,
> Islanded by cities fair ;
> Underneath Day's azure eyes
> Ocean's nursling, Venice, lies,
> A peopled labyrinth of walls,
> Amphitrite's destined halls,
> Which her hoary sire now paves
> With his blue and beaming waves.
> Lo ! the sun upsprings behind,
> Broad, red, radiant, half-reclined
> On the level quivering line
> Of the waters crystalline ;
> And before that chasm of light,
> As within a furnace bright,
> Column, tower, and dome, and spire,
> Shine like obelisks of fire,

Pointing with inconstant motion
From the altar of dark ocean
To the sapphire-tinted skies ;
As the flames of sacrifice
From the marble shrines did rise,
As to pierce the dome of gold,
Where Apollo spoke of old.

PERCY BYSSHE SHELLEY.

No sound is uttered,—but a deep
　　And solemn harmony pervades
The hollow vale from steep to steep,
　　And penetrates the glades.
Far distant images draw nigh
Called forth by wondrous potency
Of beamy radiance, that imbues
Whate'er it strikes with gem-like hues.
In vision exquisitely clear
　　Herds range along the mountain side ;
　　And glistening antlers are descried ;
And gilded flocks appear.
Thine is the tranquil hour, purpureal eve !
　　But long as god-like wish, or hope divine,
Informs my spirit, ne'er can I believe
　　That this magnificence is wholly thine.
From worlds not quickened by the sun
A portion of the gift is won ;
An intermingling of Heaven's pomp is spread
On ground which British shepherds tread.

WILLIAM WORDSWORTH.

A sunrise and a setting . . . both supernatural ;
for Shelley vaguely so, in terms of a classical allusion ;
for Wordsworth definitely and unequivocally. The

29

supernaturalness of that transfiguring evening hour, which he renders with such precision and force, is an article of Wordsworth's metaphysical faith.

The horizontal light of evening causes the world to shine with such an unusual, such a goldenly improbable radiance, that, looking, we are startled out of our ordinary purblind complacency ; we are almost forced to see things as they really are and not as we imagine them to be. Or rather, since we cannot see things as they really are, we are forced to become aware of our immediate impressions and to forget the phantom generalizations and symbols which constitute our everyday universe.

Hence the supernaturalness of evening.

Those British shepherds in the last line come very near to blighting, retrospectively, the whole of Wordsworth's poem. Words change their meaning and, still more, their flavour. In Wordsworth's day, ' British ' was primarily associated with King Arthur and Boadicea and the Druids. Its flavour was romantic, antiquarian. The self-conscious imperialism which has made it, for modern palates, so extremely distasteful, had not yet been thought of. To-day, the romantic, antiquarian word would be ' English.' We are justified in emending the last line accordingly.


What's that which, ere I spake, was gone ?
So joyful and intense a spark
That, whilst o'erhead the wonder shone,
The day, before but dull grew dark ?

I do not know ; but this I know,
    That, had the splendour lived a year,
The truth that I some heavenly show
    Did see, could not be now more clear.

This too I know ; might mortal breath
    Express the passion then inspired,
Evil would die a natural death,
    And nothing transient be desired.

And error from the soul would pass,
    And leave the senses pure and strong
As sunbeams.  But the best, alas !
    Has neither memory nor tongue.

COVENTRY PATMORE.

The night is full of stars, full of magnificence ;
    Nightingales hold the wood, and fragrance loads the
        dark.
    Behold what fires august, what lights eternal !  Hark !
What passionate music poured in passionate love's
    defence.
Breathe but the wafting wind's nocturnal frankincense !
    Only to feel this night's great heart, only to mark
    The splendours and the glooms, brings back the
        patriarch
Who on Chaldaean wastes found God through reverence.

Could we but live at will upon this perfect height,
    Could we but always keep the passion of this peace,
Could we but face unshamed the look of this pure light,
    Could we but win earth's heart and give desire release,
Then were we all divine, and then were ours by right
These stars, these nightingales, these scents ; then shame
        would cease.

LIONEL JOHNSON.

31

What wondrous life is this I lead !
Ripe apples drop about my head ;
The luscious clusters of the vine
Upon my mouth do crush their wine ;
The nectarine and curious peach
Into my hands themselves do reach ;
Stumbling on melons, as I pass
Ensnared with flowers, I fall on grass.
Meanwhile the mind from pleasure less
Withdraws into its happiness ;
The mind, that ocean, where each kind
Does straight its own resemblance find ;
Yet it creates, transcending these,
Far other worlds and other seas,
Annihilating all that's made
To a green thought in a green shade.
Here at the fountain's sliding foot
Or at some fruit tree's mossy root,
Casting the body's vest aside,
My soul into the boughs does glide ;
There like a bird it sits and sings,
Then whets and combs its silver wings ;
And, till prepared for longer flight,
Waves in its plumes the various light.

ANDREW MARVELL.

Par les soirs bleus d'été j'irai dans les sentiers,
Picoté par les blés, fouler l'herbe menue ;
Rêveur, j'en sentirai la fraîcheur à mes
        pieds,
Je laisserai le vent baigner ma tête nue.
Je ne parlerai pas, je ne penserai rien,
Mais l'amour infini me montera dans l'âme ;

Et j'irai loin, bien loin, comme un bohémien,
Par la Nature—heureux, comme avec une femme.
ARTHUR RIMBAUD.


Summer ends now ; now, barbarous in beauty, the
    stooks rise
Around ; up above, what wind-walks ! what lovely
    behaviour
Of silk-sack clouds ! has wilder, wilful-wavier
Meal-drift moulded ever and melted across skies ?
I walk, I lift up, I lift up heart, eyes,
Down all that glory in the heavens to glean our
    Saviour ;
And eyes, heart, what looks, what lips yet gave you a
Rapturous love's greeting of realer, of rounder
    replies ?
And the azurous hung hills are his world-wielding
    shoulder
Majestic—as a stallion stalwart, very-violet-sweet !—
These things, these things were here and but the
    beholder
Wanting ; which two when they once meet,
The heart rears wings bold and bolder
And hurls for him, O half hurls earth for him off
    under his feet.            GERARD MANLEY HOPKINS.


In a letter to Hawthorne, Herman Melville has
written well of these country ecstasies. His remarks
arise out of a discussion of Goethe's philosophy.
    'Here is a fellow with a raging toothache. "My
dear boy," Goethe says to him, "you are sorely
afflicted with that tooth ; but you must *live in the All*,
and then you will be happy !" As with all great
                                                        33

genius, there is an immense deal of flummery in Goethe.
. . . *P.S.*—This " all " feeling, though, there is some
truth in. You must often have felt it, lying on the grass
on a warm summer's day. Your legs seem to send out
shoots into the earth. Your hair feels like leaves upon
your head. This is the " *all* " feeling. But what plays
the mischief with the truth is that men will insist upon
the universal application of a temporary feeling or
opinion.'

The trouble is that we can never, in the nature of
things, do anything else. All ' feelings and opinions '
are temporary ; they last for a while and are then
succeeded by other ' feelings and opinions.' Thus, it
is only very occasionally that we observe a phenomenon
like the Brownian movement. Indeed, the vast
majority of people have never observed it at all. But
men of science feel justified in making universal applica-
tions of the ' temporary feeling ' they have during their
occasional observations and in basing upon it a whole
theory of molecular behaviour. And this despite of
the fact that they, along with the rest of mankind, live
their daily lives with the intimate conviction that
molecules not only don't move, but don't exist. The
*all* feeling is brief and occasional ; but this is not to say
that a metaphysical system based upon it must necessarily be untrue. Nor does the great predominance in
our lives of not-all feelings necessarily invalidate an all-
theory, any more than a theory of molecular movement is invalidated by our almost constant sense of the
solidity and stability of matter. It is only in certain
special circumstances that we can observe the Brownian

movement ; at other times we observe stillness. Similarly, it is only in special circumstances that we have the all-feeling ; at other times we have an immediate sense of separateness. We cannot help it ; we are made that way. Melville is quite right, of course, in insisting that this immediate sense of separateness cannot be denied ; an all-philosophy will not cure toothache, just as the molecular theory will not modify our native incapacity to be aware of molecules. On the other hand, toothache (Melville's expressive symbol of separateness) and the non-molecular life are, on their own plane, undeniable realities. Our experience is divided up into island universes. We jump from one to the other—there are no bridges. Because of their peculiar quality, we say that some of these experiences are more real, or at any rate more significant than others. But the others, nevertheless, continue to exist. We cannot ' always keep the passion of this peace ' ; and ' the best, alas, has neither memory nor tongue.' It is only of a god that Patmore could write (in that rather disquietingly emphatic style of his) :—

> The whole of life is womanhood to thee,
> Momently wedded with enormous bliss.

For mortals, a great deal of their lives is manhood and wild beasts and mud.

> To fly from, need not be to hate mankind :
> All are not fit with them to stir and toil,
> Nor is it discontent to keep the mind
> Deep in its fountain, lest it overboil

35

In the hot throng, where we become the spoil
Of our infection, till too late and long
We may deplore and struggle with the coil,
In wretched interchange of wrong for wrong
Midst a contentious world, striving where none are
    strong.

Is it not better, then, to be alone,
And love Earth only for its earthly sake ?
By the blue rushing of the arrowy Rhone,
Or the pure bosom of its nursing lake,
Which feeds it as a mother who doth make
A fair but froward infant her own care,
Kissing its cries away, as these awake ;—
Is it not better thus our lives to wear
Than join the crushing crowd, doomed to inflict or
    bear ?

I live not in myself, but I become
Portion of that around me ; and to me
High mountains are a feeling, but the hum
Of human cities torture : I can see
Nothing to loathe in nature, save to be
A link reluctant in a fleshly chain,
Classed among creatures, when the soul can flee,
And with the sky, the peak, the heaving plain
Of ocean, or the stars, mingle, and not in vain.

And thus I am absorbed, and this is life :
I look upon the peopled desert past,
As on a place of agony and strife,
Where, for some sin, to sorrow I was cast,
To act and suffer, but remount at last
With a fresh pinion, which I feel to spring,
Though young, yet waxing vigorous as the blast

Which it would cope with, on delighted wing,
Spurning the clay-cold bonds which round our being
    cling.

And when at length the mind shall be all free
From what it hates in this degraded form,
Reft of its carnal life, save what shall be
Existent happier in the fly and worm,
When elements to elements conform
And dust is as it should be, shall I not
Feel all I see, less dazzling, but more warm ?
The bodiless thought ?   The Spirit of each spot ?
Of which, even now, I share at times the immortal
    lot ?                              LORD BYRON.


Wherein lies happiness ?   In that which becks
Our ready minds to fellowship divine,
A fellowship with essence ;   till we shine,
Full alchemized and free of space.   Behold
The clear religion of heaven !   Fold
A rose leaf round thy finger's taperness
And soothe thy lips ;  hist, when the airy stress
Of music's kiss impregnates the free winds,
And with a sympathetic touch unbinds
Aeolian magic from their lucid wombs :
Then old songs waken from enclouded tombs ;
Old ditties sigh above their father's grave ;
Ghosts of melodious prophesyings rave
Round every spot where trod Apollo's foot ;
Bronze clarions awake, and faintly bruit,
Where long ago a giant battle was ;
And, from the turf, a lullaby doth pass
In every place where infant Orpheus slept.

Feel we these things ?—that moment have we stepped
Into a sort of oneness, and our state
Is like a floating spirit's.  But there are
Richer entanglements, enthralments far
More self-destroying, leading by degrees
To the chief intensity ;  the crown of these
Is made of love and friendship and sits high
Upon the forehead of humanity.
All its more ponderous and bulky worth
Is friendship, whence there ever issues forth
A steady splendour ;  but at the tip-top
There hangs by unseen film an orbèd drop
Of light, and that is love :  its influence
Thrown in our eyes genders a novel sense
At which we start and fret ;  till in the end,
Melting into its radiance, we blend,
Mingle, and so become a part of it,—
Nor with aught else can our souls interknit
So wingedly ;  when we combine therewith,
Life's self is nourished by its proper pith,
And we are nurtured like a pelican brood.
Ay, so delicious is the unsating food,
That men, who might have towered in the van
Of all the congregated world, to fan
And winnow from the coming step of time
All chaff of custom, wipe away all slime
Left by men-slugs and human serpentry,
Have been content to let occasion die,
Whilst they did sleep in love's Elysium.
And, truly, I would rather be struck dumb
Than speak against this ardent listlessness :
For I have ever thought that it might bless
The world with benefits unknowingly ;

As does the nightingale, up-perchèd high,
And cloistered among cool and bunchèd leaves—
She sings but to her love, nor e'er conceives
How tip-toe Night holds back her dark grey hood.
Just so may love, although 'tis understood
The mere commingling of passionate breath,
Produce more than our searching witnesseth :
What I know not : but who, of men, can tell
That flowers would bloom, or that green fruit would
    swell
To melting pulp, that fish would have bright mail,
The earth its dower of river, wood, and vale,
The meadows runnels, runnels pebble-stones,
The seed its harvest, or the lute its tones,
Tones ravishment, or ravishment its sweet,
If human souls did never kiss and greet ?

JOHN KEATS.

Perhaps separateness is really an illusion, perhaps there is, after all, some mysterious unity. Ontologically and absolutely, the ' all-philosophy ' may be true. Or it may be false. As with all ontological problems, there is really no knowing. One thing, however, is certain : in spite of the toothache, Goethe's advice is sound ; the best way to be happy is to try to live out of personal separateness, in the all—to try to share, in Byron's words, ' the immortal lot ' of the spirit of things, to form, in Keats's, ' a fellowship with essence.'

Our ordinary day-to-day existence is that of a separate being having contact with his own abstractions from, and generalizations about, the world revealed to him by his sensations and intuitions. At certain moments, this separate being goes behind the abstractions and generalizations and becomes directly conscious of his sensations and intuitions—an apocalyptic process, which Keats describes (in terms which have as much or as little meaning as most philosophical language) as the forming of a fellowship with essence.

For all of us, the most intolerably dreary and deadening life is that which we live in ourselves. Happiness is to ' become portion of that around me '—portion of the *essence* of that around me, Keats would qualify. We are happy only when the self achieves union with the not-self. Now both self and not-self are states of our consciousness. External nature can seem to us either all too natural—a boring projection of our own boring selves—or else when we get behind our abstractions and generalizations, supernatural, an unearthly not-self with which, however, we can unite our being so that, like it, we are all not-self. The arrowy Rhone and the mountains, the sea, sky, stars—all these are valuable in so far as they stimulate us to exchange the consciousness of separate selfhood for that of not-self, essence, the all. (The names are many, but the experience, the state of awareness, is only one.)

Keats finds in love a stimulus to ' all-feelings '—a stimulus of the same kind as external nature, but more eminent in degree. Nature is good ; but in love

> there are
> Richer entanglements, enthralments far
> More self-destroying, leading by degrees
> To the chief intensity.

40

Love, for Keats, is the quintessence of the not-self ;
and yet, by a seeming paradox,

> when we combine therewith,
> Life's self is nourished by its proper pith,
> And we are nurtured like a pelican brood.

The not-self is the very core and marrow of our
beings.

Of the other stimuli to ' all-feelings ' and a consciousness of the not-self, Keats does not speak in this
passage from ' Endymion.' Intellectual, ethical,
mystical, even sensual, they exist and are, according
to circumstances and the temperament of those on
whom they act, more or less efficacious, more or less
completely satisfying. This is not, however, the place
to discuss them.

Grands bois, vous m'effrayez comme des cathédrales,
Vous hurlez comme l'orgue, et dans nos cœurs
    maudits,
Chambres d'éternel deuil où vibrent de vieux râles,
Répondent les échos de vos *De Profundis.*

Je te hais, Océan ! tes bonds et tes tumultes,
Mon esprit les retrouve en lui ! Ce rire amer
De l'homme vaincu, plein de sanglots et d'insultes,
Je l'entends dans le rire énorme de la mer.

Comme tu me plairais, ô Nuit ! sans ces étoiles
Dont la lumière parle un langage connu !
Car je cherche le vide, et le noir, et le nu !

Mais les ténèbres sont elles-mêmes des toiles
Ou vivent, jaillissant de mon œil par milliers,
Des êtres disparus, aux regards familiers !

CHARLES BAUDELAIRE

The essential horror of Baudelaire's existence was that he could never, for all the intensity of his longing, break out from the prison of self into the happy freedom of the not-self. He wanted to have the ' all-feeling,' to ' share the immortal lot ' of the spirit of things, to establish a ' fellowship with essence.' But he always remained narrowly, hopelessly, mortally himself. Instead of becoming ' portion of that around him,' he assimilated external nature to himself. To Byron, high mountains were a feeling—an ' all-feeling ' ; to Baudelaire, they and the woods, the sea, the night, were as much a torture as the hum of human cities. Everything spoke *un langage connu*. The world was part of his tortured spirit and his sick body ; never, even for a moment, could they become a part of the impersonal world.

# THE INDIVIDUAL

DESCEND, O Lamb of God, and take away the im-
  putation of Sin
By the creation of States and the deliverance of
  individuals evermore, Amen.
Thus wept they in Beulah over the four regions of
  Albion :
But many doubted and despaired and imputed Sin
  and righteousness,
To Individuals and not to States, and these slept in
  Ulro.

WILLIAM BLAKE.

Affections, Instincts, Principles and Powers,
Impulse and Reason, Freedom and Control—
So men, unravelling God's harmonious whole,
Rend in a thousand shreds this life of ours.
Vain labour ! Deep and broad, where none may
  see,
Spring the foundations of the shadowy throne
Where Man's one nature, queen-like, sits alone,
Centred in a majestic unity ;
And rays her powers, like sister islands, seen
Linking their coral arms under the sea ;
Or clustered peaks, with plunging gulfs between
Spanned by aerial arches, all of gold,
Where'er the chariot wheels of life are rolled
In cloudy circles, to eternity.

MATTHEW ARNOLD.

I am gall, I am heartburn.   God's most deep decree
Bitter would have me taste :  my taste was me ;

43

Bones built in me, flesh filled, blood brimmed the curse.
Selfyeast of spirit a dull dough sours.  I see
The lost are like this, and their scourge to be
As I am mine, their sweating selves ;  but worse.

GERARD MANLEY HOPKINS.

For the *homme moyen sensuel*, Blake's doctrine of states is one of the most alluring ever propounded.  Accepted, it frees us at one stroke from all moral responsibility whatsoever.

According to Blake's theory, the individual is no longer accountable for his actions.  Responsibility can be attached only to states and not to the person (if such a being any longer exists) who passes through the states.  The individual self is reduced to a mere locality in space—the region where states occur ;  nothing more. There is no need for any of us to sleep in Ulro—to suffer, that is to say, the pains of hell, whether posthumously or in the form of present remorse.  What a comfort !

But a question arises.  How far does the doctrine square with observable facts ?  To what extent, if we happen to be intellectually honest, can we accept it ?

Certain facts are clearly unamenable to interpretation in terms of Blake's theory.  To start with, we have bodies—bodies which retain through gradual change an unmistakable individual identity.  In the second place, the ' bitter taste of me ' is something with which each one of us is only too familiar.  But ' self is an illusion.'  Possibly ;  it is an illusion, however, which lasts a lifetime and is shared by all human beings. My mind has never been subtle enough to see much difference between such illusions and reality.  I am a

44

fact of my own immediate experience. But the
illusion, or the reality of self is not quite unbroken. It
has holes in it, so to speak, rifts and flaws. I am a fact
of my own experience ; but so, occasionally, is not-I.
For the bitter taste of self is not continuously on our
palate. There are times when we forget it ; times when
some other savour seems for a moment to take its place ;
times when we are conscious of being something other
than our ordinary selves—better, worse, inhumanly
vaster or inhumanly more limited. Of the possible
significance of certain of these abnormal experiences I
have allowed the poets to speak in other sections of this
book. What concerns us here is the fact that we do
really have them, that we sometimes actually feel and
*taste* ourselves to be other than we ordinarily are. Even
the law recognizes the existence of these abnormal
states. By admitting, as in most countries it does, a
distinction between crimes of passion and crimes of
calculation, it admits that men are sometimes not themselves—it ' imputes sin and righteousness to states ' and
so preserves the offending individual from sleeping in
Ulro, to say nothing of swinging from the gallows.

Blake's doctrine, then, would seem to be partially
true. Our successive states are islands—but, for the
most part, ' sister islands linking their coral arms under
the sea ' ; islands of the same archipelago, having the
same geology, the same fauna and flora, the same
climate and civilization. But here and there, in mid-
ocean, rises some isolated peak ; uninhabited, or
peopled by races of strange men and unknown animals ;
an island where life is unrecognizably different from

45

that which we lead on the familiar atolls of our home waters. Between these and the oceanic islands, there exists, no doubt, some obscure, submarine connection. If in no other way, they are at least united in this : that they rise from the crust of the same globe. But the connection is invisible ; we have no direct knowledge of it, can only infer its existence. For practical purposes—as mystics and lawyers unexpectedly agree—it is not there.

In describing these islands, the psychological geographer may lay his chief emphasis either on the sea that sunders them, or on the linked coral arms under the sea. It is less a matter of scientific accuracy (for, as we have seen, man is simultaneously a diversity of states *and* an individual unity) than of taste and expediency. Individual responsibility is the essence of all existing systems of ethics ; therefore moralists have always insisted on the submarine connections. The imputation of sin and righteousness to states is subversive, not only of morality, but of all organized society. If a man is nothing but a succession of states, then contracts, property, social position are without justification or even meaning. Suppose, for example, my state A makes an agreement with your state X. A week later state B has succeeded to state A and state Y to state X. If there are no coral arms under the sea, if we impute sin and righteousness only to states—then, clearly, there is no reason why the old agreement should be binding on the new states. We may try to wriggle out from under the burden of sin and righteousness ; but simple expediency demands that we should ·impute business arrangements to individuals rather than to states.

46

Over against the moralist and the business man, stand the immoralist and the psychological analyst—geographers, who emphasize the sea as opposed to the coral. Immoralists may be of the transcendental kind —men beyond good and evil, like certain mystics, Blake among them—or else quite ordinary misbehavers anxious to evade responsibility for their offences. The transcendental immoralists provide the crowd of untranscendental average sensual men with a justifying doctrine. Hence the popularity of Blake at the present time. The religious bases of the traditional morality were long ago destroyed ; and now after hanging for some time miraculously suspended in air, the morality itself has begun to crumble. Blake seems to offer a justifying explanation for behaviour that would otherwise be merely lawless and animal.

The psychological analyst is inevitably, whatever his intentions happen to be, on the side of the immoralists. Analysis is an insistence on separation. The analyst perceives divisions in what had seemed continuous, fissures through what others, less keen-eyed, had thought the solid earth.

Under his pen, two islands grow where only one grew before. He is perpetually recognizing new states, emphasizing the distinction between those already known. In the modern novel psychological analysis has been carried to a point never reached before. With what results ? That ' characters,' in the accepted sense of the word, have disappeared, to be replaced by a succession of states. We know each state very well ; but what precisely is the sum of the states ? what, finally, is

47

the character of the man under analysis ? Of that, as analysis goes further and further, we become less and less certain.

Writing of Stendhal, Professor Saintsbury speaks of ' that psychological realism, which is perhaps a more different thing from psychological reality than our clever ones for two generations have been willing to admit or, perhaps, able to perceive.' Joyce, Proust and a host of minor writers have carried the realistic analysis many stages further than it was taken in *Le Rouge et le Noir*. And the ' psychological reality ' of individualized characters has correspondingly grown dimmer.

What has happened in the realm of psychology is analogous to what has happened in the realm of physics. The physicist who analyses any common object of sensuous experience comes at last to a sub-atomic universe not merely quantitatively, but even qualitatively different from the macroscopic world of daily life. The laws of nature which hold good when we are dealing with billions of atoms do not apply when we are dealing with thousands or unities. A table is radically different from the atoms of which it is composed.

Some such difference seems to hold between characters and the individual states into which they can be analysed. We can look at human beings macroscopically or microscopically, with the eye of Shakespeare or the eye of Lawrence. Thanks to the psychological research-workers, it is possible for us to see ourselves and our fellows as individuals or as successive states—and therefore as morally responsible for what we do, or as morally irresponsible.

# MAN AND NATURE

For, oh ! is it you, is it you,
Moonlight, and shadow, and lake,
And mountains, that fill us with joy,
Or the poet who sings you so well ?
Is it you, O beauty, O grace,
O charm, O romance, that we feel,
Or the voice which reveals what you are ?
Are ye, like daylight and sun,
Shared and rejoiced in by all ?
Or are ye immersed in the mass
Of matter, and hard to extract,
Or sunk at the core of the world,
Too deep for the most to discern ?
Like stars in the deep of the sky,
Which arise on the glass of the sage,
But are lost when their watcher is gone.

MATTHEW ARNOLD.

The world, like an ore-bearing mountain, is veined
with every possible kind of significance. We are all
miners and quarrymen, tunnelling, cutting, extracting.
An artist is a man equipped with better tools than those
of common men—sometimes, too, with a divining rod
by whose aid he discovers, in the dark chaotic mass,
veins of hitherto unsuspected treasure—new meanings
and values. He opens our eyes for us, and we follow in
a kind of gold rush. The whole world seems all at once
to glitter with the nuggets which he first taught us to
see. What was empty of significance becomes, after
his passage, suddenly full—and full of *his* significance.

49

Nature, as Wilde insists in one of the best of his essays, is always imitating art, is perpetually creating men and things in art's image. How imperfectly did mountains exist before Wordsworth ! How dim, before Constable, was English pastoral landscape ! Yes, and how dim, for that matter, before the epoch-making discoveries of Falstaff and the Wife of Bath, were even English men and women !

Nations are to a very large extent invented by their poets and novelists. The inadequacy of German drama and the German novel perhaps explains the curious uncertainty and artificiality of character displayed by so many of the Germans whom one meets in daily life.

Thanks to a long succession of admirable dramatists and novelists, Frenchmen and Englishmen know exactly how they ought to behave. Lacking these, the Germans are at a loss. It is good art that makes us natural.

> Nature has no outline, but Imagination has.
> Nature has no tune, but Imagination has.
> Nature has no supernatural, and dissolves.
> Imagination is eternity.
>
> WILLIAM BLAKE.

At Altamira and in the painted caves of the Dordogne there are palaeolithic bisons that might have been drawn by Degas. On the walls of the rock shelters of a later age there are neolithic figures of men and animals that might have been drawn by a child of seven. And yet all the evidence conclusively shows that the men of the New Stone Age were incomparably more intelligent

50

and accomplished than their Magdalenian ancestors. The seeming degeneration of neolithic art is in fact an advance. For it marks an increase in the power of generalization. When he drew his bisons, the palaeolithic medicine man was simply putting an outline round his visual memories. The neolithic artist worked in a different way. What he set down was a set of hieroglyphical symbols, each representing an intellectual abstraction. A circle—that stood for Head ; an egg for Body ; four lines for Arms and Legs.

Neolithic man, it is evident, had learned to think mainly in words—real conceptual words, not mere noises expressive of emotional states. Apes have emotional noises, but no names for classes of objects. The language of palaeolithic man was probably not very unlike the language of apes. He must have found it difficult to make noises when emotionally calm. (An unexcited dog cannot bark.) Noises that were intellectual abstractions—these he was only just learning to make. His power of generalization was therefore extremely feeble. He thought in terms of particular images. Hence the snapshot realism of his bisons—a realism which is only recaptured when men, grown very highly civilized, discover a technique for forgetting that art of abstraction, which made civilization possible, and learn to look at the world once again with the unprejudiced eyes of beings who do not yet know how to speak. Nature, then, does not change ; but the outlines that man sees in Nature, the tunes he hears, the eternities he imaginatively apprehends—these, within certain limits, are continuously changing.

51

Of thee, kind boy, I ask no red and white
  To make up my delight,
  No odd becoming graces,
Black eyes, or little know-not-whats in faces ;
Make me but mad enough, give me good store
Of love for her I court,
  I ask no more ;
'Tis love in love that makes the sport.

There's no such thing as that we beauty call ;
  It is mere cozenage all ;
  For though some long ago
Liked certain colours mingled so and so,
That doth not tie me now from choosing new ;
  If I a fancy take
  To black and blue,
That fancy doth it beauty make.

'Tis not the meat, but 'tis the appetite
  Makes eating a delight ;
  And if I like one dish
More than another, that a pheasant is.
What in our watches, that in us is found,
  So to the height and nick
  We up be wound,
No matter by what hand or trick.

SIR JOHN SUCKLING.

How admirable is the colloquial ease of the seventeenth century ! These high-spirited gentlemen talked
in their natural voices, and it was poetry. The art died
with them and has never since been recovered.

> 'Tis not the meat, but 'tis the appetite
> Makes eating a delight.

This is true. But it is also true that, our physiology being what it is, there are some foods which we simply cannot relish.

> If I a fancy take
> To black and blue,
> That fancy doth it beauty make.

Suckling puts his argument in the conditional. *If*. But in point of actual fact it is almost infinitely improbable that he will take a fancy to black and blue. Nature and second nature have limited him to white and gold, to olive and black, to sunburn and chestnut. Arguments based on conditional clauses lose their persuasive force when we discover that the conditions are never likely to be fulfilled. There are values which persist, because there is a physiology which persists and, along with a physiology, a mental structure.

HECTOR

Brother, she is not worth what she doth cost
The holding.
                    TROILUS
          What is aught but as 'tis valued ?

HECTOR

But value dwells not in particular will ;
It holds his estimate and dignity
As well wherein 'tis precious in itself
As in the prizer. 'Tis mad idolatry
To make the service greater than the god ;
And the will dotes that is inclinable
To what infectiously itself affects,
Without some image of the affected merit.

WILLIAM SHAKESPEARE.

53

Things may be said to be ' precious in themselves ' in so far as all men have similar bodies, together with minds that, for all their immense variety, still preserve certain common characteristics. To any class of objects, like valuers will tend to attribute like values. For practical purposes, these persistent values may be regarded as ' absolute ' and the valued things as ' precious in themselves.'

The ancient tradition that the world will be consumed in fire at the end of six thousand years is true, as I have heard from Hell.

For the cherub with the flaming sword is hereby commanded to leave his guard at the tree of life ; and when he does, the whole creation will be consumed and appear infinite and holy, whereas it now appears finite and corrupt.

This will come to pass by an improvement of sensual enjoyment.

But first the notion that man has a body distinct from his soul is to be expunged ; this I shall do by printing in the infernal method, by corrosives, which in Hell are salutary and medicinal, melting apparent surfaces away, and displaying the infinite which was hid.

If the doors of perception were cleansed, everything would appear to man as it is, infinite.

For man has closed himself up, till he sees all things through narrow chinks of his cavern.

WILLIAM BLAKE.

The implication here is that our imaginations can create the world in their own image. That they do some creating is obvious. But it is surely no less obvious that there is a limit to their powers. Blake himself half admits it. *If* the doors of perception are cleansed, and *if* sensual enjoyment is improved, then the world will appear infinite and holy. And, in point of fact, artists and mystics do succeed, from time to time and for a brief moment, in cleansing their perception and improving their sensual enjoyment—with the happiest effects on the world in which they live. But experience shows that the processes of cleansing and improvement cannot go beyond a certain point, and that the effects cannot last for more than a very short time. We are not free to create imaginatively a world other than that in which we find ourselves. That world is given. For either, as common sense affirms, there is a thing in itself outside and independent of our consciousness, a thing which is unchangeably what it is, and so limits the creative power of the imagination in just the same way as his material limits the power of the sculptor. Or else subjective idealism is true and we create our world, but create it by means of a certain type of mind which, as it can only vary within relatively narrow limits, can only project a certain narrowly varying kind of universe. Blake wants the world to be different from what it is and asserts that, by some miracle, it will become different. And in the first moment of reading we generally believe him, because he is a great and most persuasive artist, and because what he says is always partly true and wholly desirable. No philosopher is quite so exciting as Blake ; for none has the art of mingling such profound and

55

important truths with such beautiful, wish-fulfilling errors. Add the finest poetry, or a magnificently gnomic prose, and you have a mixture that turns the strongest heads.

However, there are also mornings after. For me, to-day is one of them. I have slept off my dose of Blake and write sober.

Mes bouquins refermés sur le nom de Paphos,
Il m'amuse d'élire avec le seul génie
Une ruine, par mille écumes bénie
Sous l'hyacinthe, au loin, de ses jours triomphaux.

Coure le froid avec ses silences de faulx,
Je n'y hululerai pas de vide nénie
Si ce très blanc ébat au ras du sol dénie
A tout site l'honneur du paysage faux.

Ma faim qui d'aucuns fruits ici ne se régale
Trouve en leur docte manque une saveur égale :
Qu'un éclate de chair, humain et parfumant !

Le pied sur quelque guivre où notre amour tisonne,
Je pense plus longtemps peut-être éperdûment
A l'autre, au sein brûlé d'une antique amazone.
STÉPHANE MALLARMÉ.

When the 'studied lack' of fruits begins to have a savour equal to that of the fruits themselves, and the Amazon's absent breast seems more desirable than the unamputated flesh of real women—then, surely, it is time to sound the alarm. Incapable of re-creating, except in patches and for transient moments, the world of objective reality, disappointed imagination elaborates a paradise of private and onanistic satisfactions. The

process, if kept within due bounds, is salutary enough.
Men need compensations and occasional holidays ;
must keep their spirits up by taking, from time to time,
a fancied vengeance on the stubborn and recalcitrant
world. But to make a system, a regular philosophy of
onanism—this is appalling. And this, precisely, is what
the Symbolists and some of the earlier Romantics deliberately did. The religion of imagination is a dangerous faith, liable to the most deplorable corruptions.
But, all the same, how lovely Mallarmé's sonnet is !
How profoundly satisfying ! Images new and yet
inevitable ; not an otiose word, but every phrase precise, concentrated, pregnant with significance ; the
sentences winding with a serpentine logic into the
understanding, falling on the imagination with the
rich musical thunder of enchantments and magic spells.
Here is a small, but absolute perfection.

> O Lady ! we receive but what we give,
> And in our life alone does Nature live :
> Ours is her wedding-garment, ours her shroud !
>    And would we aught behold, of higher worth
> Than that inanimate cold world, allowed
> To the poor loveless, ever-anxious crowd,
>    Ah ! from the soul itself must issue forth
> A light, a glory, a fair luminous cloud
>    Enveloping the earth—
> And from the soul itself must there be sent
>    A sweet and potent voice, of its own birth,
> Of all sweet sounds the life and element.
>
>              SAMUEL TAYLOR COLERIDGE.

Coleridge is wrong. There are moments when we

receive more and other things than those we give. For
the most part, of course, we impose our moods on the
world without us ; and not our moods only, our
humanity, our mode of being. Incorrigibly anthropomorphic, man insists on trying to live in a man-like
world. And in civilized countries, and under a
temperate sky, he is pretty successful. In the home
counties of England, for example, Nature seems to most
people, and for most of the time, reassuringly human—
all too human, even. But every now and then something startling happens. For one reason or another
Nature suddenly refuses to live with our life and partake
of our moods. She turns round on the human spectator
and gives him something utterly unlike his gift to her,
reveals herself as a being either marvellously and
beautifully, or else, more often, terrifyingly alien from
man. In one of the finest passages of ' The Prelude '
Wordsworth has recorded this most disquieting experience. I quote it at length.

Dust as we are, the immortal spirit grows
Like harmony in music ; there is a dark
Inscrutable workmanship that reconciles
Discordant elements, makes them cling together
In one society. How strange that all
The terrors, pains and early miseries,
Regrets, vexations, lassitudes interfused
Within my mind, should e'er have borne a part,
And that a needful part, in making up
The calm existence that is mine, when I
Am worthy of myself ! Praise to the end !
Thanks to the means which Nature deigned to employ ;
58

Whether her fearless visitings, or those
That came with soft alarm, like hurtless light
Opening the peaceful clouds ; or she may use
Severer interventions, ministry
More palpable, as best might suit her aim.

One summer evening (led by her) I found
A little boat tied to a willow tree
Within a rocky cave, its usual home.
Straight I unloosed her chain, and stepping in
Pushed from the shore.   It was an act of stealth
And troubled pleasure, nor without the voice
Of mountain echoes did my boat move on ;
Leaving behind her still, on either side,
Small circles glittering idly in the moon,
Until they melted all into one track
Of sparkling light.   But now, like one who rows,
Proud of his skill, to reach a chosen point
With an unswerving line, I fixed my view
Upon the summit of a craggy ridge,
The horizon's utmost boundary ;  far above
Was nothing but the stars and the grey sky.
She was an elfin pinnace ;  lustily
I dipped my oars into the silent lake,
And, as I rose upon the stroke, my boat
Went heaving through the water like a swan ;
When, from behind that craggy steep, till then
The horizon's bound, a huge peak, black and huge,
As if with voluntary power instinct,
Upreared its head.   I struck and struck again,
And growing still in stature the grim shape
Towered up between me and the stars, and still,
For so it seemed, with purpose of its own
And measured motion like a living thing,

Strode after me.  With trembling oars I turned,
And through the silent water stole my way
Back to the covert of the willow tree :
There in her mooring-place I left my bark,—
And through the meadows homeward went in grave
And serious mood ;  but after I had seen
That spectacle, for many days my brain
Worked with a dim and undetermined sense
Of unknown modes of being ;  o'er my thoughts
There hung a darkness, call it solitude
Or blank desertion.  No familiar shapes
Remained, no pleasant images of trees,
Of sea or sky, no colours of green fields ;
But huge and mighty forms, that do not live
Like living men, moved slowly through the mind
By day, and were a trouble to my dreams.

WILLIAM WORDSWORTH.

Very few ' nature poets ' have had the courage to
admit that their goddess lives with an unknown mode
of being, that she sometimes reveals herself, unequivocally as the most terrifying and malignantly alien of
deities.  Wordsworth himself spent a great deal of time
and energy trying to hush up the scandal.  But he was
too truthful to suppress all the unfavourable evidence.
Symbolically, that huge black peak rises appalling from
the midst of his beauty spots.  Even in the best kept of
rich manorial flower gardens the goddess, as Tennyson
knew, could be darkly sinister.

The air is damp and hushed and close
As a sick man's room, when he taketh repose
    An hour before death ;

My very heart faints and my whole soul grieves
At the moist rich smell of the rotting leaves
   And the breath
Of the fading edges of box beneath
And the year's last rose.
   Heavily hangs the broad sunflower
     Over its grave i' the earth so chilly ;
   Heavily hangs the hollyhock,
     Heavily hangs the tiger-lily.
ALFRED, LORD TENNYSON.

## To a Fish

You strange, astonished-looking, angle-faced,
Dreary-mouthed, gaping wretches of the sea,
Gulping salt water everlastingly,
Cold-blooded, though with red your blood be graced,
And mute, though dwellers in the roaring waste ;
And you, all shapes beside, that fishy be—
Some round, some flat, some long, all devilry,
Legless, unloving, infamously chaste :—

O scaly, slippery, wet, swift, staring wights,
What is't ye do ?  What life lead ?  Eh, dull
   goggles ?
How do ye vary your vile days and nights ?
How pass your Sundays.  Are ye still but joggles
In ceaseless wash ?  Still nought but gapes, and bites,
And drinks, and stares, diversified with boggles ?

## A Fish replies

Amazing monster ! that, for aught I know,
With the first sight of thee didst make our race
For ever stare !  O flat and shocking face,
Grimly divided from the breast below !

61

Thou that on dry land horribly dost go
With a split body and most ridiculous pace,
Prong after prong, disgracer of all grace,
Long-useless-finned, haired, upright, unwet, slow !

O breather of unbreathable, sword-sharp air,
How canst exist ?  How bear thyself, thou dry
And dreary sloth ?   What particle canst share
Of the only blessed life, the watery ?
I sometimes see of ye an actual *pair*
Go by, linked fin by fin, most odiously.

*The Fish turns into a Man, and then into a Spirit,*
*and again speaks*

Indulge thy smiling scorn, if smiling still,
O man !  and loathe, but with a sort of love ;
For difference must its use by difference prove,
And, in sweet clang, the spheres with music fill.
One of the spirits am I, that at his will
Live in whate'er has life—fish, eagle, dove—
No hate, no pride, beneath nought, nor above,
A visitor of the rounds of God's sweet skill.

Man's life is warm, glad, sad, 'twixt loves and graves,
Boundless in hope, honoured with pangs austere,
Heaven-gazing ;  and his angel-wings he craves :—
The fish is swift, small-needing, vague yet clear,
A cold, sweet, silver life, wrapped in round waves,
Quickened with touches of transporting fear.

LEIGH HUNT.

The world below the brine,
Forests at the bottom of the sea—the branches and
    leaves.
Sea-lettuce, vast lichens, strange flowers and seeds—

the thick tangle, the openings, and the pink turf,
Different colours, pale grey and green, purple, white
and gold—the play of light through the water,
Dumb swimmers there among the rocks—coral,
gluten, grass, rushes—and the aliment of the
swimmers,
Sluggish existences grazing there, suspended, or
slowly crawling close to the bottom :
The sperm-whale at the surface blowing air and spray
or disporting with his flukes,
The leaden-eyed shark, the walrus, the turtle, the
hairy sea-leopard, and the sting-ray,
Passions there, wars, pursuits, tribes—sight in those
ocean depths—breathing that thick breathing
air, as so many do.
The change thence to the sight here, and to the
subtle air breathed by beings like us, who walk
this sphere :
The change onwards from ours to that of beings who
walk other spheres.

WALT WHITMAN.

The queer, the dubious, the not-quite-right—in a
word, the fishy.

Popular imagination has always recognized the
peculiar remoteness of fish. Cats, dogs, horses, mice,
cows—these have, or seem to have, something human
about them. But fish—no ! Each time we catch a fish
we draw up out of the sinister subaqueous world a
piece of pure strangeness. The fish is for us an emblem
of that beautiful, terrifying and incomprehensible
universe in which (though we contrive, most of the
time, to ignore the fact) we have our precarious being.

63

Leviathan and Behemoth are God's emblems for grand occasions ; fish are the celestial heraldry for ordinary days.

These three sonnets of Leigh Hunt—by far the best things their author ever wrote—render with an extraordinary subtlety, beauty and precision, the essential strangeness of fish and their significance for us as symbols of other modes of being than our own. Less intensely and sharply, with a heavier eloquence, Whitman expresses the same idea. Most ' nature poets ' unjustifiably moralize and humanize the object of their worship. Hunt's ' legless, unloving, infamously chaste ' monsters come with a salutary reminder that the world is, after all, unmoral. Whitman's ' sluggish existences grazing there ' on the pink turf startle us into realizing what familiarity with our surroundings too often makes us forget—that nature is incredibly foreign to us and that one of the main ' points ' of her, so far as we are concerned, consists precisely in this disquieting and stimulating inhumanity.

# MAN AND BEHEMOTH

Thou art indeed just, Lord, if I contend
With thee ; but, sir, so what I plead is just.
Why do sinners' ways prosper ? and why must
Disappointment all I endeavour end ?
Wert thou my enemy, O thou my friend,
How wouldst thou worse, I wonder, than thou dost
Defeat, thwart me ?   Oh, the sots and thralls of lust
Do in spare hours more thrive than I that spend,
Sir, life upon thy cause.   See, banks and brakes
Now, leavèd how thick ! lacèd they are again
With fretty chervil, look, and fresh wind shakes
Them ; birds build—but not I build ; no, but strain,
Time's eunuch, and not breed one work that wakes.
Mine, O thou lord of life, send my roots rain.

                                    GERARD MANLEY HOPKINS.

The necessary ignorance of man explains to us
much ; it shows us that we could not be what we
ought to be, if we lived in the sort of universe we should
expect.   It shows us that a latent Providence, a confused life, an odd material world, an existence broken
short in the midst are not real difficulties, but real
helps ; that they, or something like them, are essential
conditions of a moral life to a subordinate being.

                                    WALTER BAGEHOT.

Are they shadows that we see ?
And can shadows pleasure give ?
Pleasures only shadows be,
Cast by bodies we conceive,
And are made the things we deem
In those figures which they seem.

But these pleasures vanish fast
Which by shadows are exprest.
Pleasures are not if they last ;
In their passage is their best ;
Glory is most bright and gay
In a flash, and so away.

Feed apace, then, greedy eyes,
On the wonder you behold :
Take it sudden as it flies,
Though you take it not to hold :
When your eyes have done their part,
Thought must length it in the heart.

SAMUEL DANIEL.

Oh, wearisome condition of humanity !
  Born under one law, to another bound ;
Vainly begot, and yet forbidden vanity ;
  Created sick, commanded to be sound ;
    What meaneth Nature by these diverse laws ?
    Passion and Reason, self-division's cause.

Is it the mark or majesty of power
  To make offences that it may forgive ?
Nature herself doth her own self deflower
  To hate those errors she herself doth give.
    But how should man think what he may not do,
    If Nature did not fail, and punish too ?

Tyrant to others, to herself unjust,
  Only commands things difficult and hard.
Forbids us all things which it knows we lust,
  Makes easy pains, impossible reward.
    If Nature did not take delight in blood,
    She would have made more easy ways to good.

We that are bound by vows and by promotion,
  With pomp of holy sacrifice and rites,
To lead belief in good and still devotion,
  To preach of heaven's wonders and delights ;
    Yet when each of us in his own heart looks,
    He finds the God there far unlike his books.

                       FULKE GREVILLE.

         O cruel goddes, that governe
This world with binding of your word eterne,
And wryten in the table of adamaunt
Your parlement and your eterne graunt,
What is mankinde more unto you holde
Than is the sheep that rouketh in the folde ?
For slayn is man right as another beste,
And dwelleth eke in prison and arreste,
And hath siknesse and great adversitee,
And ofte times gilteless, pardee !
What governaunce is in this prescience
That gilteless tormenteth innocence ?
And yet encreaseth this all my penaunce,
That man is bounden to his observaunce,
For Goddes sake, to letten of his wille,
Ther as a beste may al his lust fulfille.
But when a beste is dead, he hath no peyne ;
But man after his death moot wepe and pleyne,
Though in this world he have care and woe.

                    GEOFFREY CHAUCER.

Never, I think, has the just man's complaint against
the universe been put more forcibly, worded more tersely
and fiercely than in Hopkins's sonnet. God's answer
is to be found in that most moving, most magnificent
and profoundest poem of antiquity, the Book of Job.

67

Man and the universe are incommensurable. Leviathan and Behemoth—these are the heraldic beasts of God. The universe is vast, beautiful and appalling ; by all our human standards monstrous ; but, precisely because of its monstrousness, divine and to be worshipped. And if the nature of things were not a Behemoth, if it treated the just man according to his merits, where would those merits be ? They would be nowhere. Just as ' pleasures are not if they last,' so virtues are not if they are rewarded. In a humanly acceptable universe, as Bagehot has pointed out in the admirable essay from which I have quoted, the just man would be non-existent. For the essence of virtue is disinterestedness. But there could be no disinterested-ness in a world which automatically rewarded virtue and punished vice. Men would be good by conditioned reflex and calculation. In other words, they would not be good at all. There can be no humanity except in an inhuman world, no virtue except against a background of Behemoths and Leviathans.

An unpleasant background ; and the condition of humanity is wearisome indeed. And perhaps, Chaucer suggests, the gods are deliberately cruel ; perhaps Behemoth is not brainless but consciously malevolent. But this, surely, is to pay the monster too high a compliment.

# EARTHLY PARADISE

Whenas the rye reach to the chin,
And chopcherry, chopcherry ripe within,
Strawberries swimming in the cream,
And schoolboys playing in the stream ;
Then, O, then, O, then, O, my true love said,
Till that time come again,
She could not live a maid.

GEORGE PEELE.

Now the lusty spring is seen :
   Golden yellow, gaudy blue
   Daintily invite the view.
Everywhere, on every green,
Roses blushing as they blow
   And enticing men to pull,
Lilies whiter than the snow,
   Woodbines of sweet honey full :
      All love's emblems, and all cry :
      ' Ladies, if not plucked, we die ! '

Yet the lusty spring has stayed :
   Blushing red and purest white
   Daintily to love invite
Every woman, every maid.
Cherries kissing as they grow,
   And inviting men to taste,
Apples even ripe below,
   Winding gently to the waist :
      All love's emblems, and all cry :
      ' Ladies, if not plucked, we die ! '

JOHN FLETCHER.

In an arbour green, asleep whereas I lay,
The birds sang sweet in the middès of the day ;
I dreamèd fast of love and play :
    In youth is pleasure, in youth is pleasure.

R. WEVER.

For that same sweet sin of lechery, I would say as
the Friar said : A young man and a young woman in
a green arbour in a May morning—if God do not
forgive it, I would.

SIR JOHN HARINGTON.

It is better to love two too many than one too few.

SIR JOHN HARINGTON.

      Spatiari dulce est
      per loca nemorosa ;
      dulcius est carpere
      lilia cum rosa ;
      dulcissimum est ludere
      cum virgine formosa !

ANON.

Venus, and young Adonis sitting by her,
Under a myrtle shade began to woo him ;
She told the youngling how god Mars did try her,
And as he fell to her, so fell she to him.
' Even thus,' quoth she, ' the wanton god embraced
    me ! '
And then she clasped Adonis in her arms !
' Even thus,' quoth she, ' the warlike god unlaced
    me ! '
As if the boy should use like loving charms.
But he, a wayward boy, refused the offer,
And ran away, the beauteous queen neglecting ;

70

Showing both folly to abuse her proffer,
And all his sex of cowardice detecting.
   O that I had my mistress at that bay,
   To kiss and clip me till I ran away !
BARTHOLOMEW GRIFFIN.

     Cupid, pardon what is past,
     And forgive our sins at last !
     Then we will be coy no more,
     But thy deity adore ;
     Troths at fifteen will we plight,
     And will tread a dance each night
     In the fields, or by the fire,
     With the youths that have desire.
     Given ear-rings will we wear,
     Bracelets of our lovers' hair
     Which they on their arms shall twist,
     With their names carved, on our wrist ;
     All the money that we owe
     We in tokens shall bestow ;
     And learn to write that, when 'tis sent,
     Only our loves know what is meant ;
     O, then pardon what is past,
     And forgive our sins at last !
BEAUMONT AND FLETCHER.

O for a bowl of fat canary,
Rich Aristippus, sparkling sherry !
Some nectar else from Juno's dairy ;
O these draughts would make us merry !

O for a wench !  I deal in faces
And in other daintier things ;
Tickled I am with her embraces ;
Fine dancing in such fairy rings !

71

O for a plump, fat leg of mutton !
Veal, lamb, capon, pig and coney !
None is happy but a glutton,
None an ass but who wants money.

Wines, indeed, and girls are good ;
But brave victuals feast the blood ;
For wenches, wine and lusty cheer
Jove would come down to surfeit here.

THOMAS MIDDLETON.

And who has seen a fair alluring face,
    A lusty girl yclad in quaint array,
Whose dainty hand makes music with her lace,
    And tempts thy thoughts, and steals thy sense
        away ;

Who has beheld fair Venus in her pride
    Of nakedness, all alabaster white,
In ivory bed, strait laid by Mars his side,
    And hath not been enchanted by the sight ;

To wish to dally and to offer game,
    To coy, to court, et cetera to do ;
(Forgive me, Chasteness, if in terms of shame,
    To thy renown, I paint what 'longs thereto.)

GEORGE PEELE.

Music and poetry is his delight ;
Therefore I'll have Italian masques by night,
Sweet speeches, comedies and pleasing shows.
And in the day, when he shall walk abroad,
Like sylvan nymphs my pages shall be clad ;
My men like satyrs, grazing on the lawns,
Shall with their goat-feet dance the antic hay ;
Sometimes a lovely boy in Dian's shape,

With hair that gilds the water as it glides,
Crownets of pearl about his naked arms,
And in his sportful hands an olive tree,
To hide those parts which men delight to see,
Shall bathe him in a spring ; and there, hard by,
One like Actæon, peeping through the grove,
Shall by the angry goddess be transformed
And, running in the likeness of a hart,
By yelping hounds pulled down shall seem to die.

CHRISTOPHER MARLOWE.

So fair a church as this had Venus none :
The walls were of discoloured jasper-stone,
Wherein was Proteus carved ; and overhead
A lively vine of green sea-agate spread,
Where by one hand light-headed Bacchus hung,
And with the other wine from grapes out-wrung.
Of crystal shining fair the pavement was ;
The town of Sestos called it Venus' glass :
There might you see the gods in sundry shapes
Committing heady riots, incest, rapes ;
For know that underneath this radiant floor
Was Danae's statue in a brazen tower ;
Jove slily stealing from his sister's bed
To dally with Idalian Ganymede,
And for his love, Europa, bellowing loud,
And tumbling with the Rainbow in a cloud ;
Blood-quaffing Mars heaving the iron net,
Which limping Vulcan and his Cyclops set ;
Love kindling fire to burn such towns as Troy ;
Silvanus weeping for the lovely boy
That now is turned into a cypress tree,
Under whose shade the wood gods love to be.

CHRISTOPHER MARLOWE.

The Elder Breughel once painted a picture of the Land of Cockayne. Viewed in its purely formal aspects, this picture may be described as a study of three recumbent figures, their heads meeting in the centre of the canvas, their legs splayed out in a star-pattern into three of its corners. Plates, a round table, loaves and pasties are arranged round them in a con-stellation of variously flattened ellipses. As a com-position, curious and interesting. But as a vision of paradise, how unsatisfactory!

Looking at the three gorged and unbuttoned Cockayners, you know that they stink of onions and stale alcohol ; that, asleep, they snore, disgustingly ; and that when they wake, their conversation will be gross and profoundly tedious. Breughel's Cockayne is a swinish paradise. But then, after all, refinement and elegance are not exactly the qualities you would expect to find in a Flemish kermesse.

The perfect, the completely acceptable vision of the earthly paradise was seen and beautifully set down by Piero di Cosimo in that enchanting *Mars and Venus* now at Berlin. Naked, the two immortally young creatures lie—Mars lightly sleeping, Venus just awake enough to be conscious of the perfection of the moment's happiness —in the foreground of a mythological-Mediterranean landscape of surpassing loveliness. Three *putti*, in the middle distance, are playing with Mars' discarded armour ; another leans against the naked flank of Venus, gazing up into the sky in an ecstasy, a wide-eyed rapture of sensuous bliss. Near him, beautiful in its rounded, living sleekness, a white rabbit enchants

74

the eye and hints, at the same time, of the warm and silky contact of fur with flesh. And that magnificent tiger-moth that has settled on the goddess's leg—how gaily pied are its wings ! and when it wakes, when at last it moves, the passage of its hurrying, hairy feet will be, for the queen of love, an almost unbearable pleasure like the creep and tingle of a kiss, radiating out from its centre of all but pain to the very extremities of the shuddering body.

The earthly paradise, the earthly paradise ! With what longing, between the bars of my temperament, do I peer at its bright landscape, how voluptuously sniff at its perfumes of hay and raspberries, of honeysuckle and roast duck, of sun-warmed flesh and nectarines and the sea ! But the bars are solid ; the earthly paradise is always on the further side. Self-hindered, I cannot enter and make myself at home. No doubt, the landscape seems all the brighter to me for that inability, the life of the senses all the more paradisiacal. ' The mind,' says Milton,

> is its own place, and in itself
> Can make a heaven of hell, a hell of heaven.

But heaven, alas, is seldom actually experienced. The mind is its own place and its tendency is always to see heaven in some other place.

> Enough, enough, ambrosial plumèd Boy !
> My bosom is aweary of thy breath.
> Thou kissest joy
> To death.
> Have pity of my clay-conceivèd birth

75

And maiden's simple mood,
Which longs for ether and infinitude,
As thou, being God, crav'st littleness and earth !
Thou art immortal, thou canst ever toy,
Nor savour less
The sweets of thine eternal childishness,
And hold thy godhead bright in far employ.
Me, to quite other custom life-inured,
Ah, loose from thy caress !
'Tis not to be endured !
Undo thine arms and let me see the sky,
By this infatuating flame obscured.
Oh, I should feel thee nearer to my heart
If thou and I
Shone each to each respondently apart,
Like stars which one the other trembling spy,
Distinct and lucid in extremes of air.

COVENTRY PATMORE.

Cupid, being a god, craves littleness and earth ; the
mortal Psyche longs for ether and infinitude. This is
all very natural and comprehensible. But, outside the
world of mythology, it is not natural that a being endowed with what intellectuals (somewhat complacently perhaps) regard as god-like faculties, should
spend his time savouring the sweets of childishness.
Cupid in actual life is as mortal as Psyche, as rigidly
confined to one place, one time, one body. Neither his
appetite nor his childishness is etèrnal ; and it is impossible for him simultaneously to savour childishness and
to function as a god in some other psychologically or
physically distant sphere. This being so, he finds himself compelled, in spite of all his cravings for littleness
76

and earth, to stick to his godhead, such as it is, and remain aloof, remote, in ' far employ.' For Psyche, on the other hand, savouring the sweets of childishness, presents not the slightest difficulty. She may have occasional longings for ether and infinitude—and incidentally one has met many Psyches, masculine as well as feminine, who never seemed to be troubled by such longings ;—but her natural place is on earth and she is at home with littleness. The earthly paradise is peopled by Psyches. The intellectual Cupids can only look on from a distance and wish that their poor godheads were of another kind.

Mr. Hastings was an original in our age, or rather the copy of our nobility in ancient days, in hunting and not warlike times. He was low, very strong, and very active, of a reddish flaxen hair, his clothes always green cloth, and never all worth when new five pounds. His house was perfectly of the old fashion, in the midst of a large park well stocked with deer, and near the house rabbits to serve his kitchen, many fish-ponds and great store of wood and timber ; a bowling green in it, long but narrow, full of high ridges, it being never levelled since it was ploughed ; they used round sand balls and it had a banqueting-house like a stand, a large one built in a tree. He kept all manner of sport-hounds that ran buck, fox, hare, otter and badger, and hawks long and short winged ; he had a walk in the New Forest and the manor of Christ Church. This last supplied him with red deer, sea and river fish ; and indeed all his neighbours' grounds and royalties were open to him, who bestowed all his time in such sports, but what he borrowed to caress his neighbours' wives and daughters, there being not a woman in all his walks of the degree of a yeoman's wife or under, and under the age of forty, but it was extremely her fault if he were not intimately acquainted with her. This made him very popular, always speaking kindly to the husband, brother or father, who was to boot very welcome to his house whenever he came ; there he found beef pudding and small beer in great plenty, a house not so neatly kept as to shame him and his dirty shoes, the great hall strewed with marrow bones, full of hawks' perches, hounds, spaniels and terriers, the upper sides of the hall hung with the fox-skins of this and the last year's skinning, here and there a polecat intermixed, guns and keepers' and huntsmen's poles in abundance. The parlour was a large long room as properly furnished ; in a great hearth paved with brick lay some terriers and the choicest hounds and spaniels ; seldom but two of the great chairs had litters of young cats in them, which were not to be disturbed, he having always three or four attending him at dinner, and a little white round stick of fourteen inches long lying by his trencher that he might defend such meat as he had no mind to part with to them. The windows which were very large, served for places to lay his arrows, crossbows, stonebows and other such like accoutrements ; the corners of the room full of the best chose hunting and hawking poles ; an oyster table at the lower end, which was of constant use twice a day all the year round, for he never failed to eat oysters before dinner and supper through all seasons ; the neighbouring

78

town of Poole supplied him with them. The upper part of this room had two small tables and a desk, on the one side of which was a church Bible, on the other the Book of Martyrs ; on the tables were hawks' hoods, bells and such like, two or three old green hats with their crowns thrust in so as to hold ten or a dozen eggs, which were of a pheasant kind of poultry he took much care of and fed himself ; tables, dice, cards and boxes were not wanting. In the hole of the desk were store of tobacco pipes that had been used. On one side of this end of the room was the door of a closet, wherein stood the strong beer and the wine, which never came thence but in single glasses, that being the rule of the house exactly observed, for he never exceeded in drink or permitted it. On the other side was a door into an old chapel, not used for devotion ; the pulpit, as the safest place, was never wanting of a cold chine of beef, pasty of venison, gammon of bacon, or great apple pie with thick crust extremely baked. His table cost him not much, though it was very good to eat at, his sports supplying all but beef and mutton, except Friday, when he had the best sea fish he could get, and was the day that his neighbours of best quality most visited him. He never wanted a London pudding, and always sung it in with ' my part lies therein-a.' He drank a glass of wine or two at meals, very often syrup of gilliflower in his sack, and had always a tun glass without feet stood by him holding a pint of small beer, which he often stirred with a great sprig of rosemary. He was well-natured, but soon angry, calling his servants bastard and cuckoldy knaves, in one of which he often spoke the truth to his own knowledge, and sometimes in both, though of the same man. He lived to a hundred, never lost his eyesight, but always writ and read without spectacles, and got to horse without help. Until past fourscore he rode to the death of a stag as well as any.

ANTHONY COOPER,
FIRST EARL OF SHAFTESBURY.

Mr. Hastings' house is not my ideal of the earthly paradise. But how dearly I wish, all the same, that I could inhabit it, could feel at home in the great hall and enjoy those dinners at the cat-infested table ! There is a large simplicity about the Hastingesque existence, a kind of grandeur in its vigorous mindlessness, most satisfying to contemplate—though, alas, most depressing, as one knows by uncomfortable experience, to meet with in reality.

Through bars once more, and from a distance, I yearn towards the scene which Shaftesbury has painted for us. Painted with what a masterly skill ! His eye for the significant fact is unfailing. That great sprig of rosemary, for example, with which Mr. Hastings stirred his beer—how easily that might have been overlooked ! But how its omission would have spoilt the picture ! Without his rosemary, Mr. Hastings would seem to us distinctly less sympathetic. That sprig of wild incense perfumes his rather gross rustic existence—gives it a certain almost idyllic flavour. Rosemary-scented, the old hunter becomes, as it were, a figure from the mythology of some religion of nature—a Priapus of Hampshire gardens, a New Forest satyr, hairy but half divine.

Æstuans intrinsecus
ira vehementi
in amaritudine
loquar meæ menti :
factus de materia
levis elementi
similis sum folio
de quo ludunt venti.

Cum sit enim proprium
viro sapienti
supra petram ponere
sedem fundamenti,
stultus ego comparor
fluvio labenti,
sub eodem aere
nunquam permanenti.

Feror ego veluti
sine nauta navis,
ut per vias aeris
vaga fertur avis,
non me tenent vincula,
non me tenet clavis,
quæro mihi similes,
et adjungor pravis.

Via lata gradior
more juventutis,
implico me vitiis
inmemor virtutis,
voluptatis avidus
magis quam salutis,
mortuus in anima
curam gero cutis.

Præsul discretissime,
veniam te precor :
morte bona morior,
dulci nece necor,
meum pectus sauciat
puellarum decor,
et quas tactu nequeo,
saltem corde mœchor.

THE ARCHPOET.

Lived too consciously by people whose native place is on the mental plane of existence, life in the earthly paradise turns rancid and becomes strangely repulsive. The Archpoet was a person, it is obvious, of enormous intellectual ability.  Nature, that is to say, had intended him to live, in the main, mentally, not in the world of sense.  Disobeying the fundamental laws of his being, he broke through the confining bars.  These stanzas are taken from a long apology for his life in what should have been the earthly paradise.  It is an astonishingly brilliant performance—but one which fails, for all its brilliance, to do what it intended to do. So far from justifying the Archpoet in his preferences for wine, woman and song, it makes us uncomfortably feel that (at any rate while such people as he are about) wine is a poison, song a waste of time and woman a defiled defilement.  The earthly paradise is a home only for Psyches ; Cupids should never be more than passing visitors.

Take back thy gift ;
Why should a man desire in any way

To vary from the kindly race of men,
Or pass beyond the goal of ordinance
Where all should pause, as is most meet for all ?

ALFRED, LORD TENNYSON.

O why was I born with a different face ?
Why was I not born like the rest of my race ?
When I look, each one starts ! when I speak, I offend.
Then I'm silent and passive, and lose every friend.

WILLIAM BLAKE.

The answer to Tennyson's question is implied in
Blake's. Some people *are* born with different faces.
The fact is there, unescapable, and must be accepted.

That thee is sent, receyve in buxomnesse,
The wrastling for this world axeth a fal.
Her nis non hoom, her nis but wildernesse :
Forth, pilgrim, forth ! Forth, beste, out of thy stal !
Know thy countree, look up, thank God of all ;
Hold the hye wey and lat thy gost thee lede,
And trouthe shal delivere, it is no drede.

GEOFFREY CHAUCER.

O saisons, ô châteaux,
Quelle âme est sans défauts ?

O saisons, ô châteaux !

J'ai fait la magique étude
Du bonheur que nul n'élude :

O vive lui ! chaque fois
Que chante le coq gaulois.

Mais je n'aurai nulle envie,
Il s'est chargé de ma vie.

83

Ce charme ! il prit âme et corps
Et dispersa tous efforts.

Que comprendre à ma parole ?
Il fait qu'elle fuit et vole !

O saisons, ô châteaux !

ARTHUR RIMBAUD.

Oisive jeunesse
A tout asservie,
Par délicatesse
J'ai perdu ma vie.

ARTHUR RIMBAUD.

The trouble with the Archpoet was that he lacked the
*délicatesse de perdre sa vie.* (As indeed do most of us.)
Rimbaud's *délicatesse* was so great that he deliberately
lost two lives—the life of sense and the life of the in-
tellect and imagination. Lost an earthly paradise and
also (the sacrifice was greater) a mental paradise, in
order to undergo privations and misery in the tropical
hells that border the Red Sea.

Tell me, ye piebald butterflies, who poise
　　Extrinsic with intrinsic joys ;
What gain ye from such short-lived, fruitless, empty
　　toys ?

Ye fools, who barter gold for trash, report,
　　Can fire in pictures warm ? Can sport
That stings the mock-sense fill ? How low's your
　　Heaven, how short !

Go, chaffer bliss for pleasure, which is had
　　More by the beast than man ; the bad
Swim in their mirth (Christ wept, ne'er laughed) ;
　　the best are sad.　　　EDWARD BENLOWES.

84

It is a good thing that people should obey the laws of their being and, when the soul demands it, lose their lives *par délicatesse*. But that they should mechanically obey some moral drill-sergeant's order to lose their lives is by no means so desirable. Particularly when the order is justified by an untenable mythology.

I struck the board and cried, No more !
    I will abroad.
What ? shall I ever sigh and pine ?
My lines and life are free ; free as the road,
Loose as the winds, as large as store.
Shall I be still in suit ?
Have I no harvest but a thorn
To let me blood, and not restore
What I have lost with cordial fruit ?

    Sure there was wine
Before my sighs did dry it ; there was corn
Before my tears did drown it,
Is the year only lost to me ?
    Have I no bays to crown it ?
No flowers, no garlands gay ? all blasted ?
    All wasted ?
Not so, my heart ; but there is fruit,
    And thou hast hands.
    Recover all thy sigh-blown age
On double pleasures ; leave thy cold dispute
Of what is fit and not ; forsake thy cage,
    Thy rope of sands,
Which petty thoughts have made, and made to thee
    Good cable, to enforce and draw
    And be thy law,

While thou didst wink and wouldst not see.
　　Away ; take heed ;
　　I will abroad.
Call in thy death's head there ; tie up thy fears.
　　He that forbears
　　　To suit and serve his need,
　　　Deserves his load.
But as I raved and grew more fierce and wild
　　At every word,
Methoughts I heard one calling, *Child* :
And I replied, *My Lord*.

GEORGE HERBERT.

Herbert was a good Anglican.  But in this poem—
one of the finest he ever wrote and among the most
moving, to my mind, in all our literature—he makes
no parade of Christian theology.  The voice that calls
the poet back from the bars, back from his longing
contemplation of the earthly paradise, is a voice from
the depths of his own nature, not the voice of an
institution or an abstract principle.  There is no
brandishing of posthumous threats, no ugly appeal to
self-interest, no Pascalian betting on the improbable
Outsider, with his one-in-a-million chance of being
(how alarmingly !) the Winner.  No ; if Herbert replied, *My Lord*, and obediently turned his eyes away
from the flowers and cordial fruits, it was not so much
through fear of hell as from an intimate conviction that
Cockayne was no place for him and that the Being
which had summoned him was a projection of his most
real, his essential self.  That is why the poem still has
such power to move us.

## SELF TORTURE

Une nuit que j'étais près d'une affreuse juive,
Comme au long d'un cadavre un cadavre étendu,
Je me pris à songer près de ce corps vendu
A la triste beauté dont mon désir se prive.

Je me représentai sa majesté naïve,
Son regard de vigueur et de grâces armé,
Ses cheveux qui lui font un casque parfumé
Et dont le souvenir pour l'amour me ravive.

Car j'eusse avec ferveur baisé ton noble corps,
Et depuis tes pieds frais jusqu'à tes noires tresses
Deroulé le trésor des profondes caresses,

Si, quelque soir, d'un pleur obtenu sans efforts
Tu pouvais seulement, ô reine des cruelles !
Obscurcir la splendeur de tes froides prunelles.

CHARLES BAUDELAIRE.

Que les grandes beautés causent de grandes peines !
Quoiqu'on nomme l'Amour un mal délicieux,
Que leurs premiers attraits sont doux et gracieux !
Mais qu'on trouve à la fin leurs douceurs inhumaines !
Que d'aveugles désirs, de craintes incertaines,
De pensers criminels, de soins ambitieux,
Font sentir aux amants la colère des Cieux,
Et le malheureux sort des espérances vaines !

Je doute cependant si je voudrais guérir
De l'extrême bonheur dont je meurs sans mourir :
Tant l'objet est puissant qui m'a l'âme enchantée.
Je crois qu'enfin l'esclave est jaloux de ses fers,

Je crois que le vautour est doux à Prométhée,
Et que les Ixion se plaisent aux Enfers.

JEAN OGIER DE GOMBAULD.

There are tropes in Gombauld's sonnet which make one think of Philinte's in *Le Misanthrope*.

Je doute cependant si je voudrais guérir
De l'extrème bonheur dont je meurs sans mourir

is reminiscent of

Belle Philis, on désespère
Alors qu'on espère toujours.

But, after all, why shouldn't Gombauld remind one of Philinte ? When all is said, Philinte was not such a very bad poet, nor Alceste such a very good critic. Alceste's favourite poem, the old song, ' Si le Roi m'avait donné Paris sa grand'ville,' is doubtless charming in its freshness and spontaneity ; but it is not remarkable for subtlety. Whereas Philinte is at least making an attempt (not a very successful one, it is true) to distinguish and analyse.

Listening not long ago, to *Le Misanthrope* at the Comédie Française, I suddenly found myself feeling something like horror of Molière's good sense. It was so appallingly, so drearily sensible ! I pined for a bit of madness. Or at least for a recognition that madness exists and has its rights. Could good sense ever have discovered that

. . . le vautour est doux à Prométhée,
Et que les Ixion se plaisent aux Enfers ?

Or having discovered, ever have admitted this profound and terrible truth ? And Baudelaire's particular illustration of the truth—could *le bon sens* accept it as credible ? Quite apart from feeling horror (and that Jewess *is* horrible), could the sensible man even bring himself to believe in the possibility of such a thing having happened ? No. And yet such things do happen, and Prometheus loves his vulture and Ixion enjoys being in hell.

# THE NATURE OF LOVE

Now what is love, I pray thee tell?
It is that fountain and that well,
Where pleasure and repentance dwell.
It is perhaps the saucing bell
That tolls us into heaven or hell,
And this is love, as I hear tell.

ANON.

Hear, ye ladies that despise,
What the mighty love has done :
Fear examples and be wise :
  Fair Calisto was a nun :
Leda, sailing on the stream,
  To deceive the hopes of man,
Love accounting but a dream,
  Doted on a silver swan ;
    Danae in a brazen tower,
    Where no love was, loved a shower.

Hear, ye ladies that are coy,
  What the mighty love can do :
Fear the fierceness of the boy :
  The chaste moon he makes to woo ;
Vesta, kindling holy fires,
  Circled round about with spies,
Never dreaming loose desires,
  Doting on the altar dies ;
    Ilion, in a short hour, higher
    He can build, and once more fire.

JOHN FLETCHER.

There are two births : the one when light
First strikes the new awakened sense ;
The other when two souls unite,
And we must count our life from thence.
When you loved me and I loved you,
Then both of us were born anew.

WILLIAM CARTWRIGHT.

I wonder, by my troth, what thou and I
Did till we loved ? Were we not weaned till then ?
But sucked on country pleasures, childishly ?
Or snorted we in the Seven Sleepers' den ?
'Twas so. But this, all pleasures fancies be.
If ever any beauty I did see,
Which I desired, and got, 'twas but a dream of thee.

JOHN DONNE.

Passions are likened best to floods and streams :
The shallow murmur, but the deep are dumb ;
So, when affection yields discourse, it seems
The bottom is but shallow whence they come.
They that are rich in words, in words discover
That they are poor in that which makes a lover.

SIR WALTER RALEIGH.

AMETAS *and* THESTYLIS *making hay-ropes*

AMETAS

Think'st thou that this love can stand,
While thou still dost say me nay ?
Love unpaid does soon disband :
Love binds love, as hay binds hay.

THESTYLIS

Think'st thou that this rope would twine,
If we both should turn one way ?

Where both parties so combine,
Neither love will twist, nor hay.

### AMETAS

Thus you vain excuses find,
Which yourself and us delay ;
And love ties a woman's mind
Looser than with ropes of hay.

### THESTYLIS

What you cannot constant hope
Must be taken as you may.

### AMETAS

Then let's both lay by our rope
And go kiss within the hay.

ANDREW MARVELL.

If thou long'st so much to learn, sweet boy, what 'tis
    to love,
Do but fix thy thought on me, and thou shalt quickly
    prove.
  Little suit at first shall win
    Way to thy abashed desire ;
  But then will I hedge thee in,
Salamander-like, with fire !

THOMAS CAMPION.

The expense of spirit in a waste of shame
Is lust in action ; and, till action, lust
Is perjured, murderous, bloody, full of blame,
Savage, extreme, rude, cruel, not to trust ;
Enjoyed no sooner, but despised straight ;
Past reason hunted ; and, no sooner had,
Past reason hated, as a swallowed bait,
On purpose laid to make the taker mad.

Mad in pursuit and in possession so ;
Had, having, and in quest to have, extreme ;
A bliss in proof—and, proved, a very woe ;
Before, a joy proposed ; behind, a dream.
    All this the world well knows ; yet none knows
      well
    To shun the heaven that leads men to this hell.
               WILLIAM SHAKESPEARE.

Campion is right at least as often as Shakespeare.
Possession sometimes begets contempt, sometimes in-
fatuation. The successful lover may hate past reason, or
else find himself ' hedged in, salamander-like, with
fire.' It depends on circumstances and, above all, on
the temperaments of the parties concerned.


    Frate, la nostra volontà quieta
    virtù di carità, che fa volerne
    sol quel ch'avemo, e d'altro non ci asseta.
               DANTE ALIGHIERI.

Piccarda speaks in Paradise ; which only means, of
course, that she is speaking of earthly love at its best.
The quality of this highest love ' quiets our will, makes
us desire only that which we have, and gives us no
other thirst.'

# LONELINESS

*Siren Chorus*

Troop home to silent grots and caves,
  Troop home and mimic as you go
The mournful winding of the waves,
  Which to their dark abysses flow.

At this sweet hour all things beside
  In amorous pairs to covert creep ;
The swans that brush the evening tide
  Homewards in snowy couples keep.

In his green den the murmuring seal
  Close by his sleek companion lies,
While singly we to bedward steal,
  And close in fruitless sleep our eyes.

In bowers of love men take their rest,
  In loveless bowers we sigh alone ;
With bosom-friends are others blest,
  But we have none—but we have none.

                                        GEORGE DARLEY.

Those seals are absurd, but they make the poem.   We
smile as we read ;  but we are enchanted—why ?  it is
impossible to say.   For of course we know quite well
that seals don't murmur, only bleat and bark and grunt.
We know that they stink—so fearfully that Menelaus
would have died of their ὀλοώτατος ὀδμή if the friendly
nymph had not brought him ambrosia to sniff.
(For ' who,' asks Homer, ' would choose to go to bed
with a monster of the deep ? '  Only another monster.)
And yet, in spite of all this, we are charmed and de·

94

lighted. Those two sleek creatures in their connubial den make us feel for the poor lonely Sirens with an intensity of sympathy which the paired swans and the merely human couples would be, by themselves, incapable of arousing.

> Δέδυκε μὲν ἀ σελάννα
> καὶ Πληΐαδες μέσαι δέ
> νύκτες, πάρα δ' ἔρχετ' ὤρα,
> ἔγω δὲ μόνα κατεύδω.

SAPPHO.

'The moon has set, and the Pleiads ; it is the middle of the night and time passes, time passes, and I lie alone.'

Not even the best of the Chinese could have said more in so small a compass. Night, and desire, the anguish of waiting and, with it, the duller, the deeper, the more hopelessly incurable pain of knowing that every light must set, that life and love are declining, declining, inexorably westering towards the darkness—all these things are implied, how completely ! in Sappho's lines. The words continue to echo, as it were, and re-echo along yet further corridors of memory, with a sound that can never completely die away (such is the strange power of the poet's voice) till memory itself is dead.

# DESIRE

Western wind, when wilt thou blow,
The small rain down can rain ?
Christ, if my love were in my arms,
And I in my bed again !

ANON.

The wind sounds like a silver wire,
And from beyond the moon a fire
Is poured upon the hills, and nigher
The skies stoop down in their desire ;
 And isled in sudden seas of light,
 My heart, pierced through with fierce delight,
 Bursts into blossom in his sight.

My whole soul waiting silently,
All naked in a sultry sky,
Droops blinded with his shining eye :
I will possess him or will die.

ALFRED, LORD TENNYSON.

They flee from me that sometime did me seek,
 With naked foot stalking within my chamber.
Once have I seen them gentle, tame and meek
 That now are wild and do not once remember
That sometimes they have put themselves in danger
To take bread at my hand ; but now they range,
 Busily seeking in continual change.

Thanked be fortune, it hath been otherwise,
 Twenty times better ; but once especial :—
In thin array, after a pleasant guise,

When her loose gown did from her shoulders fall,
And she me caught in her arms long and small,
And there withal so sweetly did me kiss,
    And softly said, ' Dear heart, how like you this ? '

It was no dream, for I lay broad awaking.
    But all is turned now, through my gentleness,
Into a bitter fashion of forsaking,
    And I have leave to go of her goodness,
And she also to use new-fangleness,
But since that I unkindly so am served,
' How like you this ? '—what hath she now deserved ?
SIR THOMAS WYAT.

O Pandarus !  I tell thee, Pandarus—
When I do tell thee, there my hopes lie drowned,
Reply not in how many fathoms deep
They lie indrenched.  I tell thee I am mad
In Cressid's love : thou answer'st, she is fair ;
Pour'st in the open ulcer of my heart
Her eyes, her hair, her cheek, her gait, her voice ;
Handlest in thy discourse O ! that her hand,
In whose comparison all whites are ink,
Writing their own reproach ; to whose soft seizure
The cygnet's down is harsh, and spirit of sense
Hard as the palm of ploughman : this thou tell'st me,
As true thou tell'st me, when I say I love her,
But saying thus, instead of oil and balm,
Thou lay'st in every gash that love hath given me
The knife that made it.
WILLIAM SHAKESPEARE.

    I do not love thee for that fair,
    Rich fan of thy most curious hair,

97

Though the wires thereof be drawn
Finer than the threads of lawn,
   And are softer than the leaves,
   On which the subtle spinner weaves.

I do not love thee for those soft
Red coral lips I've kissed so oft ;
Nor teeth of pearl, the double guard
To speech, whence music still is heard ;
   Though from these lips a kiss being taken
   Would tyrants melt and death awaken.

I do not love thee, O my fairest !
For that richest, for that rarest
Silver pillar which stands under
Thy round head, that globe of wonder ;
   Though that neck be whiter far
   Than towers of polished ivory are.

I do not love thee for those mountains
Hilled with snow, whence milky fountains
(Sugared sweets, as syrup'd berries)
Must one day run, through pipes of cherries :
   O how much those breasts do move me !
   Yet for them I do not love thee.

I love not for those eyes, nor hair,
Nor cheeks nor lips, nor teeth so rare,
Nor for thy speech, thy neck, nor breast,
Nor for thy belly, nor the rest,
   Nor for thy hand, nor foot so small,
   But—wouldst thou know, dear sweet ? — for
     all !

THOMAS CAREW.

# DESIRE

O loaded curls, release your store
Of warmth and scent, as once before
The tingling hair did, lights and darks
Outbreaking into fiery sparks,
When under curl and curl I pried
After the warmth and scent inside,
Through lights and darks how manifold—
The dark inspired, the light controlled,
As early art embrowns the gold.

ROBERT BROWNING.


Adorables frissons de l'amoureuse fièvre,
Ramiers qui descendez du ciel sur une lèvre,
  Baisers âcres et doux,
Chutes du dernier voile, et vous, cascades blondes,
Cheveux d'or inondant un dos brun de vos ondes,
  Quand vous connaîtrons-nous ?

THÉOPHILE GAUTIER.


She, as a veil down to the slender waist,
Her unadornèd golden tresses wore
Dishevelled, but in wanton ringlets waved,
As the vine curls her tendrils—which implied
Subjection, but required with gentle way,
And by her yielded, by him best received
Yielded, with coy submission, modest pride,
And sweet, reluctant, amorous delay.

JOHN MILTON.


Hair, hair. . . . The longer, our fathers unani-
mously thought, the better. How the heart beat, as the
loosened bun uncoiled its component tresses ! And if
the tresses fell to below the waist, what admiration,

99

what a rush of concupiscence ! In many, perhaps in most, young men at the present time, long hair inspires a certain repugnance. It is felt, vaguely, to be rather unhygienic, somehow a bit squalid. Long hair has become, as it were, a non-conductor of desire ; no more does it attract the lightning. Men's amorous reflexes are now otherwise conditioned.

# PHYSICAL PASSION

There are many kinds of intense and unanalysable experiences. A violent sensation, for example ; a sudden, overpowering sentiment, say, of inward illumination or conviction. Problem : how are such experiences to be expressed ? How rendered in terms of poetry ?

Two methods present themselves. The first is the method of direct statement and description. The second is the method of symbolic evocation ; the experience is not directly named or described, but implied ; the poet makes a series of symbolic statements, whose separate significances converge, as it were, on a single point outside the poem—that point being the experience which it is desired to render. In practice, poets generally employ both methods simultaneously.

Here are four poetical renderings of the experience of physical passion, the first symbolical in the oriental manner of the Song of Solomon, the other three more or less directly descriptive.

### *Lament of Ahania*

Where is my golden palace,
Where my ivory bed ?
Where the joy of my morning hour ?
Where the sons of eternity singing
To awake bright Urizen, my king,
To arise to the mountain sport,

To the bliss of eternal valleys ;
To awake my king in the morn.
To embrace Ahania's joy
On the breadth of his open bosom ?
From my soft cloud of dew to fall
In showers of life on his harvests,
When he gave my happy soul
To the sons of eternal joy,
When he took the daughters of life
Into my chambers of love.

WILLIAM BLAKE.

## A Rapture

I will enjoy thee now, my Celia, come
And fly with me to Love's Elysium.
The giant Honour, that keeps cowards out,
Is but a masquer, and the servile rout
Of baser subjects only bend in vain
To the vast idol ; whilst the nobler train
Of valiant lovers daily sail between
The huge Colossus' legs, and pass unseen
Unto the blissful shore.   Be bold and wise,
And we shall enter ; the grim Swiss denies
   Only to fools a passage, that not know
   He is but form, and only frights in show.

Let duller eyes that look from far, draw near,
And they shall scorn what they were wont to fear.'
We shall see how the stalking pageant goes
With borrowed legs, a heavy load to those
That made and bear him ; not, as we once thought,
The seed of Gods, but a weak model, wrought
   By greedy men that seek to enclose the common
   And within private arms impale free woman.

Come, then, and mounted on the wings of love
We'll cut the fleeting air, and soar above
The monster's head, and in the noblest seat
Of those blest shades quench and renew our
    heat.
There shall the Queen of Love and Innocence,
Beauty and Nature, banish all offence
From our close ivy-twines ; there I'll behold
Thy barèd snow and thy unbraided gold ;
There my enfranchised hand on every side
Shall o'er thy naked polished ivory slide.
No curtain there, though of transparent lawn.
Shall be before thy virgin treasure drawn ;
But the rich mine, to the enquiring eye
Exposed, shall ready still for mintage lie,
And we will coin young Cupids.  There a bed
Of roses and fresh myrtles shall be spread,
Under the cooler shade of cypress groves ;
Our pillows of the down of Venus' doves,
Whereon our panting limbs we'll gently lay
In the faint respites of our amorous play ;
That so our slumbers may in dreams have leisure
To tell the nimble fancy our past pleasure,
   And so our souls, that cannot be embraced,
   Shall the embraces of our bodies taste.

Meanwhile the babbling. stream shall court the
    shore,
The enamoured chirping wood-choir shall adore
In varied tunes the deity of love ;
The gentle blasts of western wind shall move
The trembling leaves, and through the close boughs
    breathe
Still music, while we rest ourselves beneath

Their dancing shade ; till a soft murmur, sent
From souls entranced in amorous languishment,
  Rouse us and shoot into our veins fresh fire,
  Till we in their sweet ecstasy expire.

Then, as the empty bee that lately bore
Into the common treasure all her store,
Flies 'bout the painted field with nimble wing,
Deflowering the fresh virgins of the spring—
So will I rifle all the sweets that dwell
In thy delicious paradise, and swell
My bag with honey, drawn forth by the power
Of fervent kisses from each spicy flower.
I'll seize the rose-buds in their perfumed bed,
The violet knots, like curious mazes spread
O'er all the garden ; taste the ripened cherries,
The warm, firm apple, tipped with coral berries.
Then will I visit with a wandering kiss
The vale of lilies and the bower of bliss ;
And where the beauteous region doth divide
Into two milky ways, my lip shall slide
Down those smooth alleys, wearing as they go
A track for lovers on the printed snow ;
Thence climbing o'er the swelling Apennine,
Retire into the grove of eglantine,
Where I will all those ravished sweets distil
Through Love's alembic, and with chymic skill
  From the mixed mass one sovereign balm derive,
  Then bring the great elixir to thy hive.

THOMAS CAREW.

Dixerat et niveis hinc atque hinc diva lacertis
cunctantem amplexu molli fovet.  Ille repente

accepit solitam flammam, notusque medullas
intravit calor et labefacta per ossa cucurrit :
non secus atque olim tonitru cum rupta corusco
ignea rima micans percurrit lumine nimbos.

VIRGIL.

We two will rise, and sit, and walk together
Under the roof of blue Ionian weather,
And wander in the meadows, or ascend
The mossy mountains, where the heavens bend
With lightest winds, to touch their paramour ;
Or linger, where the pebble-paven shore,
Under the quick, faint kisses of the sea
Trembles and sparkles as with ecstasy,—
Possessing and possessed by all that is
Within that calm circumference of bliss,
And by each other, till to love and live
Be one :—or, at the noontide hour, arrive
Where some old cavern hoar seems yet to keep
The moonlight of the expired night asleep,
Through which the awakened day can never peep ;
A veil for our seclusion, close as night's,
Where secure sleep may kill thine innocent lights ;
Sleep, the fresh dew of languid love, the rain
Whose drops quench kisses till they burn again.
And we will talk, until thought's melody
Become too sweet for utterance, and it die
In words, to live again in looks, which dart
With thrilling tone into the voiceless heart,
Harmonizing silence without a sound.
Our breath shall intermix, our bosoms bound,
And our veins beat together ; and our lips
With other eloquence than words eclipse

The soul that burns between them, and the wells
Which boil under our being's inmost cells,
The fountains of our deepest life, shall be
Confused in Passion's golden purity,
As mountain-springs under the morning sun.
We shall become the same, we shall be one
Spirit within two frames, oh ! wherefore two ?

PERCY BYSSHE SHELLEY.

If any judgments are to be made, it is, I think, to
Blake and the symbolic method that we must hand the
apple.    Carew's Rapture is astonishingly brilliant,
sharp, high-coloured ; Shelley's tireless flow of rich,
not very precise eloquence produces, cumulatively
(this fragment from *Epipsychidion* begins at the poem's
five hundred and fortieth line) its usual effect upon the
hypnotized reader, who follows the hurrying words in a
luxurious kind of hashish or peyotl trance.    But both,
it seems to me, fail to express the essential quality of
what they describe.    In this respect Ahania's Lament
is superior to either.    By means of a series of intrinsically not very striking images Blake succeeds in
rendering all the violence and intensity, all the enormity
and supernaturalness of the erotic act.    His secret
consists in the choice, for his symbols, of images on the
cosmic  scale  of  grandeur.    ' The  sons  of  eternity
singing ' remind us of the Miltonic heaven.    ' Mountain
sport ' and ' eternal valleys '   ' my soft cloud of dew '
and  ' showers  of  life  on  his  harvests '—these  suggest
an immense and divinely luminous landscape.    With
the ' sons of eternal joy ' and ' the daughters of life ' we
are back again in the realm of angelic ecstasy.    For all
106

its apparent vagueness and remoteness, the poem expresses what it has to express with an extraordinary force and precision.

In his account of the loves of Vulcan and Venus—a pasage which Montaigne considered as the most movingly voluptuous in classical literature—Virgil resorts, at the end, to the cosmic image of lightning. But his main effect is produced by making a direct appeal to the reader's own memory. *Solitam flammam, notus calor* —he calls upon us to do the work for ourselves—to reconstruct in our own minds the familiar scenes of well-known passion. It is a curious device, but surprisingly effective.

Perhaps the best accounts of physical passion are to be found in poems which are not about profane love at all. The writings of the mystics contain amazingly precise renderings of experiences which are, at any rate superficially, indistinguishable from the erotic experience. The following lines from the *Canciones que hace el alma en la intima unión de Dios* by St. John of the Cross will serve as an example.

> ¡Oh, cauterio suave!
> ¡Oh, regalada llaga!
> ¡Oh, mano blanda ! ¡Oh, toque delicado,
> Que a vida eterna sabe,
> Y toda deuda paga!
> Matando, muerte en vida la has trocado.
>
> ¡Oh, lámparas de fuego,
> En cuyos resplandores
> Las profundas cavernas del sentido,
> Que estaba oscuro y ciego,

Con extraños primores
Calor y luz dan junto a su querido!

Here the effect is obtained by combining a direct, if
in parts somewhat exaggerated, statement of bodily
sensations—cautery, wounds, delicate contacts—with
symbolic images on the cosmic scale—eternity, death,
lightning, caverns. The following lines by Crashaw
require no comment ; they are almost embarrassingly
explicit.

Dear soul be strong !
Mercy will come ere long
And bring his bosom fraught with blessings,
Flowers of never fading graces.
To make immortal dressings
For worthy souls, whose wise embraces
Store up themselves for Him, who is alone
The spouse of virgins and the Virgin's Son.
But if the noble Bridegroom, when He come,
Shall find the loitering heart from home ;
Leaving her chaste abode
To gad abroad
Among the gay mates of the god of flies ;
To take her pleasure, and to play,
And keep the devil's holiday ;
To dance i' the sunshine of some smiling
But beguiling
Sphere of sweet and sugared lies ;
Some slippery pair
Of false, perhaps as fair,
Flattering but forswearing eyes ;
Doubtless some other heart
Will get the start

Meanwhile, and stepping in before
Will take possession of the sacred store
Of hidden sweets and holy joys ;
Words which are not heard with ears
(Those tumultuous shops of noise),
Effectual whispers, whose still voice
The soul itself more feels than hears ;
Amorous languishments, luminous trances ;
Sights which are not seen with eyes ;
Spiritual and soul-piercing glances,
Whose pure and subtle lightning flies
Home to the heart, and sets the house on fire
And melts it down in sweet desire :
Yet does not stay
To ask the windows' leave to pass that way ;
Delicious deaths, soft exhalations
Of soul ;  dear and divine annihilations ;
A thousand unknown rites
Of joys and rarefied delights ;
An hundred thousand goods, glories and graces ;
And many a mystic thing,
Which the divine embraces
Of the dear Spouse of spirits with them will bring ;
For which it is no shame
That dull mortality must not know a name.
Of all this store
Of blessings, and ten thousand more
(If when He come
He find the heart from home)
Doubtless he will unload
Himself some otherwhere,
And pour abroad
His precious sweets

On the fair soul whom first He meets,
O fair ! O fortunate ! O rich ! O dear !
O happy and thrice-happy she,
Dear selected dove
Whoe'er she be,
Whose early love
With wingèd vows
Makes haste to meet her morning Spouse,
And close with his immortal kisses ;
Happy indeed who never misses
To improve that precious hour,
And every day
Seize her sweet prey,
All fresh and fragrant as He rises,
Dropping with a balmy shower
A delicious dew of spices ;
O let the blissful heart hold fast
Her heavenly armful ; she shall taste
At once ten thousand paradises ;
She shall have power
To rifle and deflower
The rich and roseal spring of those rare sweets,
Which with a swelling bosom there she meets :
Boundless and infinite, bottomless treasures
Of pure inebriating pleasures.
Happy proof ! she shall discover
What joy, what bliss,
How many heavens at once it is
To have her God become her lover.

RICHARD CRASHAW.

It is a significant fact that so few poets should even
have tried to render the exaltations and agonies of
physical love.  But it is also significant that many who

have written of divine love should, without intending it, have given the most precise and intense poetic rendering of the erotic experience from which they so scrupulously averted their attention. Blake's comments on the relation between religion and sex deserve to be better known than they seem to be. Here, in nine astonishing lines, they are.

> The moment of desire ! the moment of desire ! the virgin
> That pines for man shall awaken her womb to enormous joys
> In the secret shadows of her chamber : the youth shut up from
> The lustful joy shall forget to generate and create an amorous image
> In the shadows of his curtains and in the folds of his silent pillow.
> Are not these the places of religion, the rewards of continence,
> The self-enjoyings of self-denial ? Why dost thou seek religion ?
> Is it because acts are not lovely that thou seekest solitude,
> Where the horrible darkness is impressed with reflections of desire ?

WILLIAM BLAKE.

# LOVE AND OBLIVION

Fœda est in coitu et brevis voluptas,
et tædet Veneris statim peractæ.
Non ergo ut pecudes libidinosæ
cæci protinus irruamus illuc ;
nam languescit amor peritque flamma ;
sed sic sic sine fine feriati
et tecum jaceamus osculantes.
Hic nullus labor est ruborque nullus :
hoc juvit, juvat et diu juvabit ;
hoc non deficit, incipitque semper.

PETRONIUS ARBITER.

## English Version

Doing, a filthy pleasure is, and short ;
And done, we straight repent us of the sport :
Let us not then rush blindly on unto it ;
Like lustful beasts, that only know to do it :
For lust will languish, and that heat decay.
But thus, thus, keeping endless holiday,
Let us together closely lie and kiss,
There is no labour, nor no shame in this ;
This hath pleased, doth please, and long will please ;
    never
Can this decay, but is beginning ever.

BEN JONSON.

Le soleil, sur le sable, ô lutteuse endormie,
En l'or de tes cheveux chauffe un bain langoureux
Et, consumant l'encens sur ta joue ennemie,
Il mêle avec les pleurs un breuvage amoureux.

112

De ce blanc Flamboiement l'immuable accalmie
T'a fait dire, attristée, ô mes baisers peureux,
' Nous ne serons jamais une seule momie
Sous l'antique désert et les palmiers heureux ! '

Mais ta chevelure est une rivière tiède,
Ou noyer sans frissons l'âme qui nous obsède
Et trouver ce Néant que tu ne connais pas.

Je goûterai le fard pleuré par tes paupières,
Pour voir s'il sait donner au cœur que tu frappas
L'insensibilité de l'azur et des pierres.
                                    STÉPHANE MALLARMÉ.


Morpheus in mentem
trahit impellentem
ventum lenem
segetes maturas,
murmura rivorum
per arenas puras,
circulares ambitus
molendinorum,
qui furantur somno
lumen oculorum.

Post blanda Veneris
commercia,
lassatur cerebri
substantia.
Hinc caligantes mira novitate
oculi nantes in palpebrarum rate,
hei quam felix transitus amoris ad soporem,
sed suavior regressus soporis ad amorem !
                              ANON., 12TH-13TH CENT.

113

The Guide of our dark steps a triple veil
Betwixt our senses and our sorrow keeps ;
Hath sown with cloudless passages the tale
Of grief, and eased us with a thousand sleeps.

Ah ! not the nectarous poppy lovers use,
Not daily labour's dull, Lethean spring,
Oblivion in lost angels can infuse
Of the soiled glory and the trailing wing.

MATTHEW ARNOLD.

*Sed sic sic sine fine feriati*—the line is one of the loveliest
in all Latin poetry and contains, what is more, the most
succinct and accurate account with which I am
acquainted of a certain almost supernatural state of
bodily and mental beatitude—the *felix transitus amoris
ad soporem.* In describing this Nirvana as a mere
*Néant*—a river of unconsciousness to drown the soul in—
Mallarmé is making, it seems to me, a rather crude
simplification. And, anyhow, are such souls as his
drownable ? Complete ' oblivion of the trailing wing '
is not so easily come by. But I print the sonnet for its
genuine Mallarméan beauty and especially for those
two astonishing lines,

' Nous ne serons jamais une seule momie
Sous l'antique désert et les palmiers heureux ! '—

lines which have for years haunted my memory with all
the inveterate persistency of an old remorse.

# VAMP

As in some countries far remote from hence,
The wretched creature destinèd to die,
Having the judgment due to his offence,
By surgeons begged, their art on him to try,
Which on the living work without remorse,
First make incision on each mastering vein,
Then staunch the bleeding, then transpierce the
  corse,
And with their balms recure the wounds again.
Then poison and with physic him restore ;
Not that they fear the hopeless man to kill,
But their experience to increase the more :—
Even so my mistress works upon my ill,
  By curing me and killing me each hour.
  Only to show her beauty's sovereign power.
                              MICHAEL DRAYTON.

One cannot perform a surgical operation when one
is drunk. Those sirens who amuse themselves by
vivisecting their lovers are generally of a frigid temperament, or if not frigid, are yet exasperatedly incapable of
finding any entire, annihilating satisfaction. Sensuality
never goes either to their heads or their hearts. Their
victims are to be pitied ; but so, even more, are they
themselves. Chronic and unescapable sobriety is a
most horrible affliction.

# RIGHT TRUE END

Whoever loves, if he do not propose
The right true end of love, he's one that goes
To sea for nothing but to make him sick :
Love is a bear-whelp born ; if we o'er-lick
Our love and force it new strange shapes to take,
We err, and of a lump a monster make.
Were not a calf a monster that were grown
Faced like a man, though better than his own ?

JOHN DONNE

## Answer to the Platonicks

So angels love ; so let them love for me !
When I'm all soul, such shall my love too be.
Who nothing here but like a spirit would do
In a short time, believe 't, will *be* one too.
But shall our love do what in beasts we see ?
Even beasts eat too, but not so well as we ;
And you as justly might in thirst refuse
The use of wine, because beasts water use.
They taste those pleasures as they do their food :
Undressed they take 't, devour it raw and crude.
But to us men Love cooks it at his fire,
And adds the poignant sauce of sharp desire.
Beasts do the same, 'tis true ; but ancient fame
Says gods themselves turned beasts to do the same.
The Thunderer who, without the female bed,
Could goddesses bring forth from out his head,
Chose rather mortals this way to create,
So much he esteemed his pleasure 'bove his state.

ABRAHAM COWLEY.

116

'Tis the Arabian bird alone
Lives chaste, because there is but one.
But had kind nature made them two,
They would like doves and sparrows do.

JOHN WILMOT, EARL OF ROCHESTER.

Spenser is our only considerable platonizer. The other poets of importance agree at bottom with John Donne. Thus all Shakespeare's heroes and heroines propose the right true end of love—a fact which I had reason, not long ago, to regret. For, writing about the future Utopia, I introduced a character who, alone in that happier world, had read Shakespeare. I wanted this person to be a platonic lover ; but, reading through the plays, I realized to my dismay that platonic love is not a subject with which Shakespeare ever deals. Even the young romantic lovers, like Romeo and Troilus, make no attempt to o'erlick their love, which duly takes the old and thoroughly familiar shape. So does that of

our general mother who, with eyes
Of conjugal attraction unreproved,
And meek surrender, half-embracing leaned
On our first father ; half her swelling breast
Naked met his, under the flowing gold
Of her loose tresses hid. He, in delight
Both of her beauty and submissive charms,
Smiled with superior love, as Jupiter
On Juno smiles, when he impregns the clouds
That shed May flowers.

'Nor turned, I ween,' adds Milton,

Adam from his fair spouse, nor Eve the rites
Mysterious of connubial love refused :

117

Whatever hypocrites austerely talk
Of purity, and place, and innocence.

Equally unmonstrous and as little platonic is the love
so lyrically sung by Shelley, by Byron with such raptures
and cynicisms. Nor, generally, do Browning's Men and
Women go to sea for nothing but to make them sick.

Had we but world enough and time,
This coyness, lady, were no crime.
We would sit down and think which way
To walk, and pass our long love's day.
Thou by the Indian Ganges' side
Shouldst rubies find ; I by the tide
Of Humber should complain. I would
Love you ten years before the flood ;
And you should, if you please, refuse
Till the conversion of the Jews.
My vegetable love should grow
Vaster than empires and more slow.
An hundred years should go to praise
Thine eyes, and on thy forehead gaze ;
Two hundred to adore each breast ;
But thirty thousand for the rest.
An age at least to every part,
And the last age should show your heart.
For, lady, you deserve this state,
Nor would I love at lower rate.
But at my back I always hear
Time's winged chariot hurrying near ;
And yonder all before us lie
Deserts of vast eternity.
Thy beauty shall no more be found ;
Nor, in thy marble vault, resound

My echoing song ; there worms shall try
That long preserved virginity ;
And your quaint honour turn to dust,
And into ashes all my lust.
The grave's a fine and private place,
But none, I think, do there embrace.
Now therefore while the youthful hue
Sits on thy skin like morning dew,
And while thy willing soul transpires
At every pore with instant fires,
Now let us sport us while we may,
And now, like amorous birds of prey,
Rather at once our time devour
Than languish in his slow-chapped power.
Let us roll all our strength and all
Our sweetness up into one ball,
And tear our pleasures with rough strife
Through the iron gates of life.
Thus, though we cannot make our sun
Stand still, yet we will make him run.

ANDREW MARVELL.

Dull sublunary lovers' love,
    Whose soul is sense, cannot admit
Absence because it doth remove
    Those things that elemented it.

But we, by a love so much refined,
    That ourselves know not what it is,
Inter-assurèd of the mind,
    Care less eyes, lips and hands to miss.

JOHN DONNE.

My love is of a birth as rare
As 'tis for object strange and high ;

It was begotten by despair
Upon impossibility.

Magnanimous despair alone
Could show me so divine a thing,
Where feeble hope could ne'er have flown,
But vainly flapped its tinsel wing.

And yet I quickly might arrive,
Where my extended soul is fixed ;
But fate doth iron wedges drive,
And always crowds itself betwixt.

Therefore the love which me doth bind,
But fate so enviously debars,
Is the conjunction of the mind
And opposition of the stars.

ANDREW MARVELL.

Absence makes for idealization—particularly when
there is an exchange of letters. The writers of love
letters are compelled to express and explain their feelings to an extent unknown to lovers who enjoy one
another's physical presence. (The desire to express
and explain turns even unseparated lovers into letter
writers.) The constant repetition of these generally
exaggerated verbal affirmations acts as an auto-
suggestion ; absent, but letter-writing, lovers tend,
therefore, to work themselves up into frenzies of love
for an unrecognizably idealized object. If this process goes too far, meeting and consummation can hardly
fail to be a horrible disappointment. One admires the
wisdom of Dante who platonically loved a memory,
while living with a perfectly solid and actual wife.

A single violet transplant,
 The strength, the colour and the size
(All which before was poor and scant)
 Redoubles still and multiplies.

When love with one another so
 Interinanimates two souls,
That abler soul, which thence doth flow,
 Defects of loneliness controls. . . .

But O, alas, so long, so far,
 Our bodies why do we forbear ?
They're ours, though we're not they ; we are
 The intelligences, they the sphere.

We owe them thanks because they thus
 Did us to us at first convey ;
Yielded their forces, sense, to us,
 Nor are dross to us, but allay.

On man heaven's influence works not so,
 But that it first imprints the air ;
So soul into the soul may flow,
 Though it to body first repair.

As our blood labours to beget
 Spirits, as like souls as it can,
Because such fingers need to knit
 The subtle knot which makes us man :

So must pure lovers' souls descend
 To affections and to faculties,
Which sense may reach and apprehend,
 Else a great prince in prison lies.

To our bodies turn we then, that so
 Weak men on love revealed may look ;

Love's mysteries in souls do grow,
But yet the body is his book.

And if some lover such as we
Have heard this dialogue of one,
Let him still mark us, he shall see
Small change when we're to bodies gone.

JOHN DONNE.

Donne, like Dante, illustrates the danger of being too
well educated. He brings philosophy and science into
his lyrics—but the philosophy and science, unfortunately, of another age. These references to spheres
and their intelligences, to blood and its animal spirits,
are incomprehensible to the ordinary twentieth-
century reader, who is forced to mug up the poet's
meaning in his editor's notes. Luckily the main point
of the poem is unobscured by references to super-
annuated science and mediæval cosmology.

Some that have deeper digged love's mine than I,
Say where his centric happiness doth 'lie.
    I have loved, and got, and told ;
But should I love, get, tell till I were old,
I should not find that hidden mystery.
    O 'tis imposture all !
And as no chymic yet th' elixir got,
    But glorifies his pregnant pot,
    If by the way to him befall
Some odoriferous thing, or medicinal,
So lovers dream a rich and long delight,
But get a winter-seeming summer's night.

Our ease, our thrift, our honour and our day,
Shall we for this vain bubble's shadow pay ?
  Ends love in this, that any man
Can be as happy as I can, if he can
Endure the short scorn of a bridegroom's play ?
  That loving wretch that swears
'Tis not the bodies marry, but the minds,
  Which he in her angelic finds,
  Would swear as justly that he hears
In that day's rude, hoarse minstrelsy, the spheres.
  Hope not for mind in women ; at their best
  Sweetness and wit, they are but Mummy possesst.

JOHN DONNE.

Abstinence sows sand all over
The ruddy limbs, the flaming hair ;
But Desire gratified
Plants fruits of life and beauty there.

In a wife I would desire
What in whores is always found—
The lineaments of gratified desire.

WILLIAM BLAKE.

The sacred lowe of weel-placed love,
  Luxuriantly indulge it ;
But never tempt th' illicit rove,
  Tho' naething should divulge it :
I waive the quantum of the sin,
  The hazard of concealing ;
But, och ! it hardens a' within,
  And petrifies the feeling.

ROBERT BURNS.

123

But from the first 'twas Peter's drift
  To be a kind of moral eunuch ;
He touched the hem of Nature's shift,
Felt faint—and never dared uplift
  The closest, all-concealing tunic.

She laughed the while, with an arch smile,
  And kissed him with a sister's kiss,
And said—' My best Diogenes,
I love you well—but if you please,
  Tempt not again my deepest bliss.

'Tis you are cold—for I, not coy,
  Yield love for love, frank, warm and true ;
And Burns, a Scottish peasant boy—
His errors prove it—knew my joy
  More, learned friend, than you.

*Bocca bacciata non perde ventura,*
  *Anzi rinnuova come fa la luna :—*
So thought Boccaccio, whose sweet words might
    cure a
Male prude like you, from what you now
    endure, a
  Low-tide in soul, like a stagnant laguna.'
                    PERCY BYSSHE SHELLEY.


' He shall see small change when we're to bodies
gone.' But women ' are but Mummy possesst.' At
different moments the feelings of even the same man
are flatly contradictory. There are occasions when
abstinence sows sand all over the spirit, as well as the
limbs—when it produces that ' low-tide in soul ' which
Shelley detected in Peter Bell-Wordsworth. There are

124

other occasions when not to abstain is as hideously desiccating. Incontinence is deplorable, says the humanistic moralist, not because it offends a hypothetical deity, but because it demonstrably ' petrifies the feeling.'

Living is an art ; and, to practise it well, men need, not only acquired skill, but also a native tact and taste.

> To measure life learn thou betimes, and know
>     Toward solid good what leads the nearest way ;
>     For other things mild Heaven a time ordains,
> And disapproves that care, though wise in show,
>     That with superfluous burden loads the day,
>     And when God sends a cheerful hour, refrains.

But the art of measuring life cannot be learned in its entirety. *Poeta nascitur, non fit.* We are all poets of living—for the most part, alas, pretty bad poets.

# POLYGAMY

I never was attached to that great sect,
Whose doctrine is, that each one should select
Out of the crowd a mistress or a friend,
And all the rest, though fair and wise, commend
To cold oblivion, though it is the code
Of modern morals, and the beaten road
Which those poor slaves with weary footsteps tread
Who travel to their home among the dead
By the broad highway of the world, and so
With one chained friend, perhaps a jealous foe,
The dreariest and the longest journey go.

True love in this differs from gold and clay,
That to divide is not to take away.
Love is like understanding, that grows bright
Gazing on many truths ; 'tis like the light,
Imagination ! which from earth and sky,
And from the depths of human phantasy,
As from a thousand prisms and mirrors, fills
The Universe with glorious beams, and kills
Error, the worm, with many a sun-like arrow
Of its reverberated lightning.   Narrow
The heart that loves, the brain that contemplates,
The life that wears, the spirit that creates
One object, and one form, and builds thereby
A sepulchre for its eternity.

Mind from its object differs most in this ;
Evil from good ; misery from happiness ;
The baser from the nobler ; the impure
And frail, from what is clear and must endure.

If you divide suffering and dross, you may
Diminish till it is consumed away ;
If you divide pleasure and love and thought,
Each part exceeds the whole ; and we know not
How much, while any yet remains unshared,
Of pleasure may be gained, of sorrow spared :
This truth is that deep well, whence sages draw
The unenvied light of hope ; the eternal law
By which those live, to whom this world of life
Is as a garden ravaged, and whose strife
Tills for the promise of a later birth
The wilderness of this Elysian earth.

PERCY BYSSHE SHELLEY.

Let us hear the words of God himself, the author
of the law and the best interpreter of his own will.

2 Sam. xii. 8. *I gave thee thy master's wives into thy
bosom . . . and if that had been too little, I would moreover have given thee such and such things.* Here there can
be no subterfuge. God gave him wives, he gave them
to the man whom he loved, as one among a number
of benefits ; he would have given him more if these
had not been enough. . . . It appears to me sufficiently established by the above arguments that
polygamy is allowed by the law of God. Lest,
however, any doubt should remain, I will subjoin
abundant examples of men whose holiness renders
them fit patterns for imitation, and who are among
the lights of our faith. Foremost I place Abraham.
. . . I say nothing of Solomon, notwithstanding his
wisdom, because he seems to have exceeded due
bounds ; although it is not objected to him that he
had taken many wives, but that he had married

127

strange women.   His son Rehoboam *desired many wives*, not in the time of his iniquity, but during the three years when he is said to have walked in the way of David.                                    JOHN MILTON.


Can that be love that drinks another as a sponge
       drinks water,
That clouds with jealousy his nights, with weeping
       all the day,
To spin a web of age around him, grey and hoary,
       dark,
Till his eyes sicken at the fruit that hangs before his
       sight ?
Such is self-love that envies all, a creeping skeleton
With lamplike eyes watching around the frozen
       marriage bed.

But silken nets and traps of adamant will Oothoon
       spread,
And catch for thee girls of mild silver, or of furious
       gold.
I'll lie beside thee on a bank and view their wanton
       play
In lovely copulation, bliss on bliss, with Theotormon:
Red as the rosy morning, lustful as the first-born
       beam,
Oothoon shall view his dear delight, nor e'er with
       jealous cloud
Come in the heaven of generous love, nor selfish
       blightings bring.
                                        WILLIAM BLAKE.


Here are three ways of asserting a predilection for polygamy.   The differences between them are significant. Shelley's way is the way of the revolutionary romantic. ' I never was attached,' he says, ' to that great sect whose doctrine is,' briefly, monogamy. It is a declaration of personal non-conformity to an unpleasant religious superstition—for that is what the word ' sect ' implies monogamy to be. A superstition which no man of good sense and decent feeling can accept.

Shelley had read his encyclopaedists ; Godwin was his master as well as his father-in-law. But Godwin's disciple was also Lord Byron's friend and equal. The rationalizing individualist was also the heir to a baronetcy and a poet—was at once an aristocrat and a man of commanding talents ; and this at a time when birth still counted and when the German theory of the rights of genius was beginning to displace the French theory of the rights of man. At the beginning of the nineteenth century a man in Shelley's position and with Shelley's gifts did not feel bound to explain and rationalize his non-conformity. He merely affirmed his disagreement with the rest of the world and passed on.

Milton is at once much more and much less modest than Shelley. Shelley says, ' I should like to be polygamous,' and leaves it at that. The desire is, in his eyes, its own justification. Not so in Milton's. Milton does not dare to be unorthodox on his own responsibility. He feels it necessary to prove by irrefutable argument that he is right and that those who call themselves orthodox are wrong. Hence these texts from the Bible. For the Bible is, by definition, always right. Milton accepts its authority. In this the militant protestant of 1650 reveals himself more humble than the aristo-

129

cratic revolutionary of 1800. But humility was never the strong point of the man who wrote : ' Nothing profits more than self-esteem founded on just and right.' Milton bows, indeed, to a higher authority, but exhibits in the act of bowing a pride which makes Shelley's self-assurance seem profoundest modesty. For Shelley's self-assurance is merely human and relative. Milton's, thanks to the Bible, is absolute and superhuman.

Milton bows to the authority of the Bible, but only in order to prove that his own taste for polygamy is also Jehovah's taste. He is never content, like Shelley, to assert his preferences ; he must always believe and make other people believe that his desires and heaven's are the same. Bored by his wife, he writes a book to demonstrate that God has no objection to divorce. The book is censured ; Milton writes another to prove that God is on the side of free speech. *Vox Miltonis, vox Dei.*

Blake occupies an intermediate position between Milton and Shelley. He has not lost the habit of justifying personal predilections in terms of mythology. But whereas Milton has to do all his justifying in terms of existing myths, Blake feels himself free to invent new ones for himself. Milton's desire for more than one woman at a time is legitimate because Solomon kept a barrackful of concubines ; Blake's, because Oothoon offers to provide her spouse with ' girls of mild silver, or of furious gold.' The substitution of Golgonooza for Jerusalem is the substitution of a private for a public myth. Individualism and subjectivism have triumphed ; the time is ripe for Shelley's simple assertion of a personal preference. ' I should like to have a number of women, not because Oothoon and Jehovah approve of polygamy, but simply because that happens to be my desire.'

That three of the most considerable of English poets should have wanted to be polygamous (Shelley was the only one of them who ever came near fulfilling his wishes) is certainly a curious fact—but though curious, not, I think, astonishing. Good artists are, as a rule, but indifferent monogamists. They tend to combine a more than ordinary sensibility, energy and curiosity with a more than ordinary reluctance to assume the responsibilities of common life.

Talent has its categorical imperatives. An artist cannot help feeling that his first duty is towards his art, and that he does wrong if he allows any but the most supremely important non-artistic considerations to stand in the way of its accomplishment.

(In his middle years Milton deliberately abandoned his artistic mission, but only for a cause which seemed, at the moment, even higher. What supported him in the years when ' these eyes their seeing had forgot ' ?

The conscience, friend, to have lost them overplied
In Liberty's defence, my noble task,
Of which all Europe rings from side to side.)

For the majority of artists, at any rate of male artists, marriage will not seem a cause sufficiently important to make sacrifices for. But marriage can be almost as much of an undertaking as the defence of liberty. For the essence of monogamous marriage consists in the assuming of responsibilities—not merely social and economic, but also, and above all, emotional. To a greater or less extent these emotional responsibilities must almost inevitably interfere with the artist's performance of his primary artistic duties. If he obeys his categorical imperatives and ignores his emotional responsibilities, he is a bad monogamist. If his emotional responsibilities are heavy and he accepts them in spite of his categorical imperatives, he is a bad artist. In practice, most artists make some sort of more or less (generally less) satisfactory compromise.

Polygamy is a state in which there are no emotional responsibilities—only emotional excitements. So far from preventing the artist from doing his aesthetic duty, polygamy may actually, by providing him with constant stimulation, make the doing of it more easy. Add to this the natural tendency of very sensitive, energetic and inquisitive men to be strongly affected by female charms and you will understand why Milton yearned back so nostalgically to Abraham and Solomon ; why Blake wanted ' handmaidens ' in the house and, when Mrs. Blake objected, wrote so feelingly of the golden girls of Golgonooza ; why Shelley not only preached polygamy in his *Epipsychidion*, but even to some extent practised it—with what generally agonizing results, the biographies duly set forth.

> If God had laid all common, certainly
>     Man would have been th' incloser ; but since now
> God hath impaled us, on the contrary
>     Man breaks the fence and every ground will
>         plough.                    GEORGE HERBERT.

## POLYGAMY

In the first ruder age, when love was wild,
Nor yet by laws reclaimed, nor reconciled
To order, nor by reason manned, but flew
Full-summed by nature, on the instant view,
Upon the wings of appetite, at all
The eye could fair or sense delightful call ;
Election was not yet ; but as their cheap
Food from the oak or the next acorn-heap,
As water from the nearest spring or brook,
So men their undistinguished females took
By chance, not choice.   But soon the heavenly spark,
That in man's bosom lurked, broke through the dark
Confusion :   then the noblest heart first felt
Itself for its own proper object melt.

THOMAS CAREW.

# MARRIAGE

My love is strengthened, though more weak in seeming ;
I love not less, though less the show appear ;
That love is merchandized, whose rich esteeming
The owner's tongue doth publish everywhere.
Our love was new, and then but in the spring,
When I was wont to greet it with my lays ;
As Philomel in summer's front doth sing,
And stops her pipe in growth of later days :
Not that the summer is less pleasant now
Than when her mournful hymns did hush the night,
But that wild music burthens every bough,
And sweets grown common lose their dear delight ;
    Therefore, like her, I sometimes hold my tongue,
    Because I would not dull you with my song.

WILLIAM SHAKESPEARE.

    Sleep on, my love, in thy cold bed
    Never to be disquieted !
    My last good night ! Thou wilt not wake
    Till I thy fate shall overtake ;
    Till age, or grief, or sickness must
    Marry my body to that dust
    It so much loves, and fill the room
    My heart keeps empty in thy tomb.
    Stay for me there ; I will not fail
    To meet thee in that hollow vale ;
    And think not much of my delay ;
    I am already on the way,
    And follow thee with all the speed
    Desire can make, or sorrows breed.

HENRY KING.

Out of the chambre hath every wight him dressed.
And Januarie hath faste in armes take
His fresshe May, his paradys, his make.
He lulleth her, he kisseth her ful ofte
With thikke bristles of his berd unsofte,
Like to the skin of houndfish, sharp as brere,
For he was shave al newe in his manere. . . .
Thus laboureth he til that the day gan dawe ;
And then he taketh a sop in fyn clarree,
And upright in his bed then sitteth he,
And after that he sang ful loude and clere,
And kiste his wyf, and made wantoun chere.
He was al coltish, ful of ragerye,
And ful of jargon as a flekked pye.
The slakke skin about his nekke shaketh,
Whyl that he sang, so chaunteth he and craketh.
But god wot what that May thoughte in her herte,
When she him saw up sittinge in his sherte,
In his night-cappe and with his nekke lene ;
She preyseth not his pleying worth a bene.

GEOFFREY CHAUCER.

What a fearful picture of marriage as it should not
be!

Chaucer was doing things before 1400 which no
other narrative artist did for nearly four centuries.
Perhaps I should have said five centuries. For, in this
tale of January and May, there are passages for which
one can find no parallel outside modern fiction. For
example, when May receives a love letter, she hurries
off, in order to read it, to the w.c. Which is, of course,
exactly where any one who wanted to be quite certain
of privacy would go. But what author before Flaubert

would have stated this obvious fact? Except for Chaucer, I can think of none.

Why should a foolish marriage vow,
    Which long ago was made,
Oblige us to each other now,
    When passion is decayed?
We loved and we loved, as long as we could,
    Till our love was loved out of us both;
But our marriage is dead, now the pleasures are fled;
    'Twas pleasure first made it an oath.

If I have pleasures for a friend
    And further love in store,
What wrong has he, whose joys did end,
    And who could give no more?
'Tis a madness that he should be jealous of me,
    Or that I should bar him of another.
For all we can gain is to give ourselves pain,
    When neither can hinder the other.

JOHN DRYDEN.

This song summarizes the whole, rather squalid philosophy of modern marriage, as expounded—at what length and in how many volumes!—by a small army of earnest publicists on either side of the Atlantic. Why do people persist in saying, yet once more, in thousands of pages, what may, as Dryden proves, be said in sixteen lines? The sole valid reason is an economic one. Only a fool would concentrate what he has to say into a poem, for which he might, with luck, get paid a guinea, when, by spreading it out thinly into eighty thousand words, he can earn several hundred pounds. One does not kill the goose that lays the golden eggs.

136

# LOVE AND LITERATURE

And what is Love ?  It is a doll, dressed up
For idleness to cosset, nurse and dandle ;
A thing of soft misnomers, so divine
That silly youth doth think to make itself
Divine by loving, and so goes on
Yawning and doting a whole summer long,
Till Miss's comb is made a pearl tiara,
And common Wellingtons turn Romeo boots ;
Then Cleopatra lives at number seven,
And Antony resides in Brunswick Square.
Fools !  if some passions high have warmed the world,
If Queens and Soldiers have played deep for hearts,
It is no reason why such agonies
Should be more common than the growth of weeds.
Fools !  make me whole again that weighty pearl
The Queen of Egypt melted, and I'll say
That ye may love in spite of beaver hats.

JOHN KEATS.

If it were not for literature, how many people would
ever fall in love ?  Precious few, I should guess.
Zuckerman has shown that even the apes and monkeys
must *learn* the sexual behaviour which is normal in
their respective communities.  Isolate a new born rat,
then, when it is mature, introduce it to another rat of
the opposite sex.  It will know exactly what to do—will
behave as all other rats behave.

Not so an ape.  Instinct does not tell it how to behave.
Congenital ignorance is the condition of intelligence.
The ape is intelligent, therefore knows fewer things by

instinct than does the rat. It is not born with a knowledge of normal sex-behaviour, it must acquire this knowledge from its fellows.

Now if the simple sexuality of an ape is an affair of education, how much more so must be the complicated love-making of men and women ! Literature is their principal teacher. Even the most wildly passionate lovers have studied in that school.

The difference between the great lovers and the Cleopatras of number seven, the Antonys of Brunswick Square, is not a difference between the untaught and the taught ; it is a difference between those who have responded wholeheartedly to their erotic education and those whose response is inadequate and forced. The latter, as Keats insists, are by far the more common.

Let us remember, however, that genuine Antonys and Cleopatras may be more numerous than would at first sight appear. No observer has any means of directly gauging the quality of other people's emotion. He can only infer it from their actions and words. The actions of people in an inconspicuous social position are mostly almost unobservable. (The number of those who can lose the world for love is at all times strictly limited.) As for their words—these are generally of a pretty poor quality. But this does not necessarily mean that the emotions they express are correspondingly poor. A talent for literary expression is rare— rarer, surely, than a talent for love. It is probable that many young consumptives have loved with agonizing intensity. What is quite certain, however, is that very, very few have written letters like Keats's to Fanny

138

Brawne. Keats is surely wrong in supposing that ordinary people—people in beaver hats—cannot love. They can—in spite of the hats, in spite of the atrociously flat and silly love letters which most of them habitually write.

Just how flat and silly the ordinary love letter is, nobody who reads the law reports in his daily paper can fail to know. The specimens there printed are almost invariably revolting in their banality. Only on the rarest occasions have I read one which I felt to be intrinsically moving. What follows—to quote one of these rare examples—is not a love letter, but a death letter, a letter written by a man just before he killed himself. The imminence of death leaves most men's style as feebly inexpressive as the burning presence of passion. The poor wretch who wrote these lines was a most exceptional suicide. Here they are.

> No wish to die. One of the best of sports, which they all knew. Not in the wrong, the boys will tell you. This b—— at Palmer's Green has sneaked my wife, one of the best in the world ; my wife, the first love in the world.

And that is all. But how moving it is ! And, in its way, how beautiful ! The rhythm of the sentences is perfect. And those repetitions at the close are managed with what, were the writer a deliberate artist, would be a most exquisite felicity. Reading this letter, we are made to feel that the man who wrote it was something more than an Antony of Brunswick Square—that the passion which made him kill himself was a genuine

139

agony on the tragical scale. But it would be possible, while preserving the sense, so to alter the phrasing of this letter that it would seem perfectly commonplace, flat, ' insincere.' We should read it with indifference and, if we thought about its author at all, say that he was a dim little man incapable of anything but a dim little suffering. And yet, in spite of beaver hats and bad style, there *is* such a thing as suicide.

# OLD AGE

Age is deformèd, youth unkind ;
We scorn their bodies, they our mind.

THOMAS BASTARD.

Things have changed since Queen Elizabeth's days.
' We,' that is to say the young, scorn not only their
bodies, but also (and above all) their minds.  In the two
politically, most ' advanced ' states of Europe this scorn
is so effective that age has become a definite bar to the
holding of political power.  Communism and Fascism
appeal for the support of youth, and of youth alone.
At Rome and Moscow age has been disfranchised.
The reasons for this state of things are simple.  In an
unchanging, or very slowly changing, environment,
old age is actually an asset.  Where the present is like
the past, a long experience of past circumstances equips
old men to deal effectually with present circumstances.
But where circumstances are rapidly changing there is
no guarantee that action which was successful in the
past will be successful in the altered present.  In a
changing world, age and long experience cease to be an
asset and become a handicap.  Hence the disfranchise-
ment of old age in Italy and Russia.

True, the leaders are trying to moderate a little the
fine scorn of the first revolutionary days.  When they
themselves were young, how lyrically they sang youth's
praises !  with what ferocious mockery they derided the
greybeards and the complacently middle-aged !  But
they themselves are now entering on middle age, and

141

the youths of a new generation are repeating with a loud and rather menacing approval the very words they themselves were using ten or twelve years ago. For how much longer will these ex-young men be successful in persuading their followers that it is essential, for the sake of the Cause, that they should continue to hold office? Within the communist society, class-war has been abolished. But, to make up for this, generation-war is just beginning. Beginning again, to be accurate ; after how many thousands of years? Among primitive peoples, a crack over the head with a club was, and still is, the equivalent of an old-age pension. Even kings had to submit to the law which condemned the old. To a white traveller who visited him, 'Give me hair-dye!' was the agonized cry of the greatest of African chiefs. 'Hair-dye!' He was going grey. Not long afterwards his warriors speared him to death. Leaders in Russia and Italy may soon expect a similar fate. They will be the first European victims of the new generation-war, which they have done so much to foster and intensify.

> Beauty is but a flower,
> Which wrinkles will devour ;
> Brightness falls from the air ;
> Queens have died young, and fair ;
> Dust hath closed Helen's eye ;
> I am sick, I must die.
>> Lord, have mercy on us !
>
> Strength stoops unto the grave ;
> Worms feed on Hector brave ;

Swords may not fight with fate ;
Earth still holds ope her gate.
Come, come, the bells do cry ;
I am sick, I must die.
    Lord, have mercy on us !

Wit with his wantonness
Tasteth death's bitterness ;
Hell's executioner
Hath no ears for to hear
What vain art can reply ;
I am sick, I must die.
    Lord, have mercy on us !

Haste therefore each degree
To welcome destiny :
Heaven is our heritage,
Earth but a player's stage.
Mount we unto the sky ;
I am sick, I must die.
    Lord, have mercy on us !

THOMAS NASHE.


Slow, slow, fresh fount, keep time with my salt tears ;
List to the heavy part the music bears,
  Woe weeps out her division when she sings.
    Droop herbs and flowers,
    Fall grief in showers,
    Our beauties are not ours ;
      O, I could still
Like melting snow upon some craggy hill,
    Drop, drop, drop, drop,
Since nature's pride is now a withered daffodil.

BEN JONSON.

Fair summer droops, droop men and beasts
    therefore;
So fair a summer look for never more ;
All good things vanish less than in a day,
Peace, plenty, pleasure, suddenly decay.
  Go not yet away, bright soul of the sad year,
  The earth is hell when thou leav'st to appear.
                     THOMAS NASHE.


One could fill volumes with this plaintive poetry of
transience. Poetry like an autumnal sunset, like bells
heard from a long way away—mournfully beautiful.
Poetry that makes us luxuriously sad. A pleasant
poetry, in spite of the threats of death and old age. For
threats, if unprecise and melodious, are almost agree-
ably moving. But melody may also be combined with
precision of statement—making it more precise. The
poet can, if he so wills, use his music to sharpen his
threats, to send them barbed and rankling into our
wincing imagination.


There was a time when, though my path was rough,
  This joy within me dallied with distress,
And all misfortunes were but as the stuff
  Whence Fancy made me dreams of happiness :
For hope grew round me, like the twining vine,
And fruits and foliage, not my own, seemed mine.
But now afflictions bow me down to earth,
Nor care I that they rob me of my mirth.
           SAMUEL TAYLOR COLERIDGE.

# OLD AGE

What is it to grow old ?
Is it to lose the glory of the form,
The lustre of the eye ?
Is it for beauty to forgo her wreath ?
—Yes, but not this alone.

Is it to feel our strength—
Not our bloom only, but our strength—decay ?
Is it to feel each limb
Grow stiffer, every function less exact,
Each nerve more loosely strung ?

Yes, this, and more ;  but not
Ah, 'tis not what in youth we dreamed 'twould be
'Tis not to have our life
Mellowed and softened as with sunset-glow,
A golden day's decline.

'Tis not to see the world
As from a height, with rapt prophetic eyes,
And heart profoundly stirred ;
And weep, and feel the fulness of the past,
The years that are no more.

It is to spend long days
And not once feel that we were ever young ;
It is to add, immured
In the hot prison of the present, month
To month with weary pain.

It is to suffer this
And feel but half, and feebly, what we feel.
Deep in our hidden heart
Festers the dull remembrance of a change,
But no emotion—none.

It is—last stage of all—
When we are frozen up within, and quite
The phantom of ourselves,
To hear the world applaud the hollow ghost
Which blamed the living man.

MATTHEW ARNOLD.

So may'st thou live, till, like ripe fruit, thou drop
Into thy mother's lap, or be with ease
Gathered, not harshly plucked, for death mature.
This is old age ; but then thou must outlive
Thy youth, thy strength, thy beauty, which will
    change
To withered, weak and grey ; thy senses then,
Obtuse, all taste of pleasure must forgo
To what thou hast ; and, for the air of youth,
Hopeful and cheerful, in thy blood will reign
A melancholy damp of cold and dry
To weigh thy spirits down, and last consume
Thy balm of life.            JOHN MILTON.

Ange plein de gaîté, connaissez-vous l'angoisse ?
La honte, le remords, les sanglots, les ennuis
Et les vagues terreurs de ces affreuses nuits
Qui compriment le cœur comme un papier qu'on
    froisse ?
Ange plein de gaîté, connaissez-vous l'angoisse ? . . .

Ange plein de santé, connaissez-vous les Fièvres ?
Qui, le long des grands murs de l'hospice blafard,
Comme des exilés, s'en vont d'un pied traînard,
Cherchant le soleil rare et remuant les lèvres ?
Ange plein de santé, connaissez-vous les Fièvres ?

146

Ange plein de beauté, connaissez-vous les rides,
Et la peur de vieillir, et ce hideux tourment
De lire la secrète horreur du devoûment
Dans des yeux où longtemps burent nos yeux avides ?
Ange plein de beauté, connaissez-vous les rides ? . . .
CHARLES BAUDELAIRE.

Coleridge writes almost prettily of what is, after all, one of the most dreadful things about old age—its insentient apathy and indifference. Who would divine, in such a pleasantly tinkling couplet as

> But now afflictions bow me down to earth,
> Nor care I that they rob me of my mirth,

the depths of infinitely depressing significance which it in fact contains ? Coleridge remains an insoluble enigma. How did so sensitive a critic and, on occasion, so magnificently successful a poet contrive, for the most part, to write such extremely inadequate verse ?— verse which utterly fails to render in terms of art the experiences which the poet was trying to express ? Unanswerable question.

Matthew Arnold's poetry often shares, though to a less extent, the defects of Coleridge's. He realized to the full and in all its details the horror of growing old ; but the actual artistic rendering of the experience, though much better than Coleridge's, is still not completely adequate. The language is oddly dead and conventional ; the versification without force and rather monotonous. (I suspect, too, that the form chosen is intrinsically unsuitable to the subject matter. Old age demands a weightier, gloomier music than can be squeezed out of blank verse lightened of half its substance and prevented, by the stanza form, from winding its way into those sustained and complicated effects which are its special glory and principal ' point ').

Milton treats the subject rather drily and perfunctorily. Dramatically, this is as it should be ; for it is an angel who thus describes the horrors of old age—a being incapable of experiencing what he so glibly talks about. Adam, thirty years later, would have spoken much more feelingly and, with Milton as his interpreter, much more movingly on the subject. As it is, the Miltonic thunders seem to rumble, in the angel's mouth, a little mechanically. We are not profoundly moved.

In Baudelaire's poem the Miltonic situation is reversed. It is not the angel who menaces man, it is man who menaces the angel—the angel who believes his youth to be everlasting, but who is in fact mortal and doomed. We are all, in our youth, that angel. Strong in the illusion of our eternity, we could laugh at the words of the man grown conscious of his mortality. Or if we wept, it was out of pure wantonness, because weeping was a change of pleasures, it is only when we are adult that we grasp the full significance of adult words.

Ange, plein de beauté, connaissez-vous les rides,
Et la peur de vieillir, et ce hideux tourment
De lire la secrète horreur du devoûment
Dans des yeux où longtemps burent nos yeux avides?

In the dark and splendid oratory of Baudelaire's third

stanza what is perhaps the worst of all the miseries of growing old finds its most accurate, its most completely adequate expression. Here are no deliciously mournful sunsets or distant bells, but a harsh pain made more agonizing by the beauty (for beauty has a penetrative force), by the grave perfection (for perfection is barbed and, having pierced, remains in the wound) of its poetical rendering.

Age is in some ways almost more appalling than death. For, in the words of Epicurus, ' when we exist there is no death, and when there is death we no more exist ' : whereas, when we are old, we still exist. Death cannot be experienced : old age can—' old age, abhorred, decrepit, unsociable, and unfriended ' ; κατάμεμπτον ἀκρατὲς ἀπροσόμιλον γῆρας ἄφιλον. The Greeks were unanimous in their horror of old age ; and it was an evil, moreover, against which they were almost defenceless. Philosophy is but a poor antidote to the miseries of age ; for that disinterested serenity of mind preached by Stoic and Epicurean alike is a product of the will. But the will is a faculty which old age, working destructively on the mind through the body, may weaken and undermine beyond all possibility of recovery. The consolations of philosophy are for the strong ; but old age is a time of weakness. Enfeebled old age looks for some source of strength outside itself. Discouraged and in decay, it asks for some abiding comfort.

(The whole subject is treated with an illuminating wealth of day-to-day clinical detail and metaphysical commentary in the *Journal Intime* of the philosopher,

Maine de Biran.  No one has written better or more scientifically than Biran on the process of growing old, none has described the influence of bodily upon mental states with more precision.  And the mind that comments on these observations is a beautiful and original mind ;  the trajectory of its development from the sensualism of Condillac to a peculiar kind of mysticism, most interesting and enlightening to follow.)

No, the Greeks, I repeat, were almost without defence against old age.  Only the votaries of the mystery religions possessed an antidote.  For they had the comforting hope of resurrection and the certainty, if they were initiates, of being, by infusion of divine grace, equal in some mysterious way to the youngest, strongest, most prosperous, superior even to the virtuous, if the virtuous happened to be uninitiated. The abiding comfort, the source of strength, the ' fruits and foliage, not their own '—these the mysteries provided.  The strong men, who found the consolations of philosophy consoling, were annoyed.  ' Diogenes,' writes Plutarch, ' may be called in to counteract Sophocles, whose lines about the Mysteries have filled innumerable minds with discouragement :—

> O thrice blest they
> That ere they pass to Hades have beheld
> These Mysteries ;  for them only, in that world,
> Is life ;  the rest have utter misery.

Diogenes, when he heard a similar statement, replied, " What do you mean ?  Is Pataikon the thief going to have a 'better lot' after death than Epaminondas, just because he was initiated?"' It is the voice of low-church good-citizenship raised against Catholicism, the voice of Kingsley protesting against Newman. And of course the protest is eminently sensible and rational. Diogenes and Charles Kingsley are quite right. But that did not, and still does not, prevent the sick, prevent the old or ageing, prevent the miserable and uneasy from running to be initiated ; or from regretting—if they cannot believe in the efficacy of sacraments, nor accept the unbelievable myths—regretting the intellectual impossibility of initiation. With the decline, perhaps only temporary, perhaps permanent, of the latest and greatest of the mystery religions, old age is becoming for us, as it was for the Greeks, the most serious of all the problems of existence. We defend ourselves against the inevitable creeping of the enemy in a variety of ways. Physiologically, first of all : the art of medicine permits us, in some measure, to postpone the onset of age and to alleviate its symptoms. By rendering the abiding consolations unnecessary, monkey gland may rob Christianity of some of its most important functions. (I use 'monkey-gland' generically to connote any rejuvenator. At the present time, church-going is certainly cheaper and may, in many cases, be more effective than Voronoff's operation.) Our next line of defence is psychological : we do not admit old age ; at a time of life when our ancestors would have been grey-beards and venerable crones, we continue to dress, talk, behave as though we were young. The old are continually auto-suggesting themselves into youthfulness. Not too unsuccessfully, in many cases.

Finally, there are our philosophical and religious defences. These, for non-Christians, are very inadequate. The consolations of philosophy are, as they always were, only for the strong. There is, as yet, little solid comfort in the thought of progressing humanity—and the religion of progressing humanity is, with the exception of a few heresies, like Christian Science, the only new religion. As for the political religion-substitutes—even at the best of times they have made little appeal to the old. And at this moment, the liveliest of them, Fascism and Communism, deliberately reject and ignore the old. Fascism, it is true, encourages them to be Catholics, if they can ; but Communism does not even allow them that resource. Old people in Russia have been robbed of all their spiritual defences without having been provided, in return, with any of the physiological defences available at any rate to the more prosperous members of our bourgeois community. Old age is bad enough anywhere ; in contemporary Russia it must be an unmitigated horror.


Ah, love, let us be true
To one another ! For the world which seems
To lie before us, like a land of dreams,
So various, so beautiful, so new,
Hath really neither joy, nor love, nor light,
Nor certitude, nor peace, nor help for pain ;
And we are here, as on a darkling plain

Swept with confused alarms of struggle and flight,
Where ignorant armies clash by night.

MATTHEW ARNOLD.

Uxor, vivamus ut viximus, et teneamus
    nomina quae primo sumpsimus in thalamo ;
nec ferat ulla dies, ut commutemur in aevo,
    quin tibi sim juvenis tuque puella mihi.

AUSONIUS.

Love, the last defence against old age—the last, and
for those whose good fortune it is to have some one
person to care for, or who have learned the infinitely
difficult art of loving all their neighbours, the best.
For it can survive, in many cases, even the ruin of
bodily and mental power, can break through the pre-
vailing insentience and apathy like a flame through
ashes. *Vivamus ut viximus* ; let us be true to one
another.

# MEMORY

Tâche donc, instrument des fuites, ô maligne
Syrinx, de refleurir aux lacs où tu m'attends !
Moi, de ma rumeur fier, je vais parler longtemps
Des déesses ; et par d'idolâtres peintures,
A leur ombre enlever encore des ceintures :
Ainsi, quand des raisins j'ai sucé la clarté
Pour bannir un regret par ma feinte écarté,
Rieur, j'élève au ciel d'été la grappe vide
Et, soufflant dans ses peaux lumineuses, avide
D'ivresse, jusqu'au soir je regarde au travers.
O nymphes, regonflons des SOUVENIRS divers.

STÉPHANE MALLARMÉ.

Ah, sad and strange, as in dark summer dawns
The earliest pipe of half-awakened birds
To dying ears, when unto dying eyes
The casement slowly grows a glimmering square ;
So sad, so strange, the days that are no more.

Dear as remembered kisses after death,
And sweet as those by hopeless fancy feigned
On lips that are for others ; deep as love,
Deep as first love and wild with all regrets ;
O Death in Life, the days that are no more.

ALFRED, LORD TENNYSON.

Life can only be understood backwards ; but it
must be lived forwards.

SÖREN KIERKEGAARD.

Remembered are in some ways lovelier than actual
goddesses ; the recollection of loosened girdles more

intoxicating than the act of loosening. It is just because they come to us wild with regret, just because we feel them to be a death in life, that memories take on their unearthly quality of sunset richness.

The mind purifies the experiences with which it is stored, composes and informs the chaos. Each man's memory is his private literature, and every recollection affects us with something of the penetrative force that belongs to the work of art.

> There was a boy ; ye knew him well, ye cliffs
> And islands of Winander ! many a time
> At evening, when the earliest stars began
> To move along the edges of the hills,
> Rising or setting, would he stand alone,
> Beneath the trees, or by the glimmering lake ;
> And there, with fingers interwoven, both hands,
> Pressed closely palm to palm, and to his mouth
> Uplifted, he, as through an instrument,
> Blew mimic hootings to the silent owls,
> That they might answer him. And they would shout
> Across the watery vale, and shout again,
> Responsive to his call,—with quivering peals,
> And long halloos, and screams, and echoes loud
> Redoubled and redoubled ; concourse wild
> Of jocund din ! And when there came a pause
> Of silence such as baffled his best skill :
> Then sometimes, in that silence, while he hung
> Listening, a gentle shock of mild surprise
> Has carried far into his heart the voice
> Of mountain torrents ; or the visible scene
> Would enter unawares into his mind
> With all its solemn imagery, its rocks,

Its woods, and that uncertain heaven received
Into the bosom of the steady lake.

WILLIAM WORDSWORTH.

The boy is spoken of in the third person, and is said
to have died before he was twelve. But I like to think
that this is a poetic fiction, and that it was really little
William himself who stood there at the lake's edge,
hooting and hooting with the indefatigable persistence
of childhood, while the yet more persistent, because
even less grown-up, owls hallooed and screamed their
answer : hoot ! halloo ! hoot, hoot, halloo !—while
the echoes bounced back and forth from wall to wall
of the mountains—hour after hour ; boy communing
with bird and both profoundly, indescribably happy ;
happy with the deep mindless happiness of living
creatures rejoicing in their life ; hour after hour, until
either some infuriated adult came out with a stick to
stop the din, or else, in a silence, as Wordsworth has
described, the child was suddenly made aware again
of his forgotten self-consciousness, his momentarily
obliterated mind and, along with these, of the outer
world and of its strangeness. And the shock, I believe,
was a shock of more than mild surprise. It was of
some obscure and nameless terror.

O litus vita mihi dulcius, O mare ! felix
 cui licet ad terras ire subinde meas !
O formosa dies ! hoc quondam rure solebam
 Naiadas alterna sollicitare manu !
Hic fontis lacus est, illic sinus egerit algas ;
 haec statio est tacitis fida cupidinibus.

156

# MEMORY

Pervixi : neque enim fortuna malignior unquam
eripiet nobis quod prior hora dedit.

PETRONIUS ARBITER.

I am always rather astonished when I find that
Romans liked their country homes, went swimming in
the sea and remembered their boyhood with pleasure.
That is the result of a liberal education. After ten years
among the best classical authors, the English schoolboy
emerges with a firm conviction of the radical non-
humanity of Greeks and Romans. Even now I receive
a sudden, pleasurable shock each time I make the discovery that they were, after all, real people. Petronius
seems rather realer than most, for the good reason
that one never read him at school.

*Pervixi* . . . The last couplet rumbles with a noble
music.

I have lived ; nor shall maligner fortune ever
Take from me what an earlier hour once gave.

But sometimes, alas, do we not wish that it would
take away our memory along with our happiness ?

Ed ella a me : ' Nessun maggior dolore
che ricordarsi del tempo felice
nella miseria : e ciò sa il tuo dottore.'

### Tired Memory

The stony rock of death's insensibility
Welled yet awhile with honey of thy love
And then was dry ;

Nor could thy picture, nor thine empty glove,
Nor all thy kind long letters, nor the band
Which really spanned
Thy body chaste and warm,
Thenceforward move
Upon the stony rock their wearied charm.
At last, then, thou wast dead.
Yet would I not despair,
But wrought my daily task, and daily said
Many and many a fond, unfeeling prayer,
To keep my vows of faith to thee from harm.
In vain.

COVENTRY PATMORE

# ENGLAND

O England, full of sin, but most of sloth !
Spit out thy phlegm and fill thy breast with glory.
Thy gentry bleats, as if thy native cloth
Transfused a sheepishness into thy story ;
   Not that they all are so, but that the most
   Are gone to grass and in the pasture lost.

                  GEORGE HERBERT.

Accurate and prophetic poet ! The gentry still
bleats. With how refined and tremulous a note ! A
baaing, not of adult ewes and rams, but of lammikins.
In Herbert's time the sheep were at least full grown.
But then the native cloth was still the genuine woollen.
To-day it is mostly viscose and acetate. Peter Pan
came in with artificial silk, his revolting uncles, the
Cheerybles, with Roberts' Self-Acting Mule. Infantil-
ism would seem to be a direct product of industrialism.

Thus from a mixture of all kinds began
That heterogeneous thing, an Englishman :
In eager rapes and furious lust begot
Between a painted Briton and a Scot ;
Whose gendering offspring quickly learnt to bow
And yoke their heifers to the Roman plough ;
From whence a mongrel half-bred race there came,
With neither name nor nation, speech or fame ;
In whose hot veins new mixtures quickly ran,
Infused between a Saxon and a Dane ;
While their rank daughters, to their parents just,
Received all nations with promiscuous lust.

This nauseous brood directly did contain
The well-extracted blood of Englishmen.

DANIEL DEFOE.

Excellent Nordic propaganda ! Defoe was, at
moments, a first-rate satirical poet. It is possible to
pick out from ' The True-Born Englishman ' a number
of admirably witty lines. Witness these on Charles II.

The royal refugee our breed restores
With foreign courtiers and with foreign whores,
And carefully repeoples us again,
Throughout the lazy, long, lascivious reign,
With such a blest and true-born English fry
As much illustrates our nobility. . . .
Six bastard dukes survive his luscious reign,
The labours of Italian Castlemaine,
French Portsmouth, Tabby Scot and Cambrian.

But the good lines lie deeply buried in a great mass of
rubbish. Like so many of even our best poets, Defoe
had very little artistic conscience.

We have offended, Oh my countrymen,
We have offended very grievously,
And been most tyrannous. From East to West
A groan of accusation pierces Heaven !
The wretched plead against us ; multitudes
Countless and vehement, the sons of God,
Our brethren. Like a cloud that travels on,
Steamed up from Cairo's swamps of pestilence,

Even so, my countrymen, have we gone forth
And borne to distant tribes slavery and pangs,
And, deadlier far, our vices, whose deep taint,
With slow perdition murders the whole man,
His body and his soul !  Meanwhile, at home,
All individual dignity and power
Engulfed in Courts, Committees, Institutions,
Associations and Societies,
A vain, speech-mouthing, speech-reporting Guild,
One Benefit-Club for mutual flattery,
We have drunk up, demure as at a grace,
Pollutions from the brimming cup of wealth.

SAMUEL TAYLOR COLERIDGE.

The modern conscience is inclined to endorse Coleridge's judgment rather than Kipling's.  Hence the
present policy in India, hence the white ruler's new
and altogether humaner attitude towards the African,
the Dyak, the Melanesian.

He is English as this gate, these flowers, this mire.
And when, at eight years old, Lob-lie-by-the-fire
Came in my books, this was the man I saw.
He has been in England as long as dove and daw,
Calling the wild cherry tree the merry tree,
The rose campion Bridget-in-her-bravery ;
And in a tender mood he, as I guess,
Christened one flower Love-in-Idleness ;
And, while he walked from Exeter to Leeds
One April, called all cuckoo-flowers Milkmaids.
For reasons of his own, to him the wren
Is Jenny Pooter.  Before all other men

F *                                           161

'Twas he first called the Hog's Back the Hog's Back.
That Mother Dunch's Buttocks should not lack
Their name was his care.   He too could explain
Totteridge and Totterdown and Juggler's Lane ;
He knows if any one.   Why Tumbling Bay
Inland in Kent is called so he might say.

EDWARD THOMAS.

# PROGRESS

The first and riper world of men and skill
Yields to our later world for three inventions ;
Miraculously we write, we sail, we kill,
As neither ancient scroll nor story mentions.
The first hath opened learnings old concealed
And obscure arts restorèd to the light ;
The second hidden countries hath revealed,
And sent Christ's Gospel to each living wight.
These we commend ; but oh, what needeth more,
To teach Death more skill than he had before !

THOMAS BASTARD.

Progress is a very recent invention. In the age of
Thomas Bastard, which was also, incidentally, the age
of Queen Elizabeth and William Shakespeare, men
believed that the race was in a state of chronic decay.
In spite of printing, the compass and gunpowder, the
earlier was considered the riper world. Those who
actually lived through what we have learnt to regard
as one of the most brilliant and progressive epochs of
all history regarded themselves as men of the decad-
ence. We, on the contrary, regard ourselves as men
of the dawn and the threshold, an army in advance,
not in retreat. It remains to be seen what the judgment
of future historians will be.

163

# ABSTRACTION

Boys and girls,
And women, that would groan to see a child
Pull off an insect's leg, all read of war,
The best amusement for our morning meal !
The poor wretch who has learned his only prayers
From curses, who knows scarcely words enough
To ask a blessing from his Heavenly Father,
Becomes a fluent phraseman, absolute
And technical in victories and defeats,
And all our dainty terms for fratricide ;
Terms which we trundle smoothly o'er our tongues
Like mere abstractions, empty sounds to which
We join no meaning and attach no form !
As if the soldier died without a wound :
As if the fibres of this godlike frame
Were gored without a pang : as if the wretch
Who fell in battle, doing bloody deeds,
Passed off to Heaven translated and not killed ;
As though he had no wife to pine for him,
No God to judge him.

SAMUEL TAYLOR COLERIDGE.

It is a pity that Coleridge's blank verse should be so very blank indeed. What he had to say was important ; but he said it inadequately. The English could have done with a memorable and mind-piercing statement of the dangers of abstraction ; alas, they have not got it. These lines contain only the raw materials for such a statement.

Without abstractions and generalizations there could

164

be no scientific knowledge. Why was there light when God said ' Let Newton be?' Because Newton did not confine his attention to the particular apple that fell on his head ; he thought about all apples, about the earth, the planets, the stars, about matter at large. Abstracting and generalizing, he illumined the entire cosmos.

The particular cases from which Newton generalized were all intrinsically insignificant. That an apple should fall is neither right nor wrong. But when a man falls, the case is altered. True, the falling man is subject to the same natural laws as the falling apple. Both have weight ; but the weight that is the man is an intrinsically significant weight. It matters a great deal whether this weight falls by accident, or is pushed, or throws itself.

There are sciences of man as well as of non-human nature. Their method is the method of all the sciences. Where they differ from the other sciences is in the fact that the particular cases from which they abstract, and upon which they base their generalizations, possess intrinsic significance. Each one is a suffering or enjoying human being.

The sciences of men are necessary and valuable. But, like many necessary and valuable things, they easily lend themselves to undesirable uses. We dislike having other people's sufferings forced on our attention, we find it very often inconvenient to have to feel compassion. To feel compassion is to feel that we are in some sort and to some extent responsible for the pain that is being inflicted, that we ought to do something about it. But most of us have no taste for doing things about anything that is not our own immediate business. To be able to think about human affairs in terms of the bodiless abstractions, the unindividualized and unmoving generalizations invented by men of science, is a real godsend. You cannot feel pity for an abstraction. Abstraction serves, accordingly, as a refuge from emotional discomfort and moral responsibility.

During wars, as Coleridge pointed out and as we all had occasion to observe, every non-combatant is a strategist—in self-defence. War is horrible, and people do not wish to be too vividly aware of the horrors. Strategy is the science of war—that is to say, a system of generalizations and abstractions, which ignores, so far as possible, the particular case. (' As if the soldier died without a wound.') Phrases like ' war of attrition ' protect the mind from contact with the particular realities of mangled flesh and putrefying corpses. They are immensely popular. The world of Platonic Ideas is the most comfortable and sanitary of dug-outs.

# HOCUS POCUS

Plain-pathed experience the unlearnèd's guide,
Her simple followers evidently shows
Sometimes what schoolmen scarcely can decide,
Nor yet wise reason absolutely knows ;
In making trial of a murder wrought,
If the vile actors of the heinous deed
Near the dead body happily be brought,
Oft 't hath been proved, the breathless corse will
    bleed.
She coming near, that my poor heart hath slain,
Long since departed, to the world no more,
The ancient wounds no longer can contain,
But fall to bleeding, as they did before.
    But what of this ?   Should she to death be led,
    It furthers justice, but helps not the dead.
MICHAEL DRAYTON.

This sonnet is, rhythmically, unusual.  Drayton has
divided every one of the first seven lines after the fifth
syllable.  The flow of the words is, in consequence,
curiously light and rapid.  The eighth line, with its
strong caesura after the fourth syllable, falls heavily
and decisively—a definite conclusion.  The versification has been effectively used to emphasize the
sense of the words.

This sense is, of course, pure nonsense—a typical
example of plain-pathed experience's wish-fulfilling
speculations about the nature of things.  The un-
learned have now become vocal ; they have a philosophy ; they justify their refusal to take the trouble

to think scientifically by an appeal to the Subconscious. Here, from a recently published volume, is a typical example of the Higher Unlearning. ' When it (the water of a certain spring) was analysed in Denver, it was said to be " highly charged with radium." That,' adds Mrs. Mabel Dodge Luhan, ' that is what we need more of on this earth, Jeffers. Radium. My instinct tells me so.' What does the instinct of the people who have contracted cancer from working with radium tell *them* ? One wonders. *Malgré tout*, I still prefer reason and experiment to plain-pathed experience and its wish-fulfilments, to even the most high-class instinct, the most appealingly feminine intuition.

# ANTI-CLERICALISM

*Sonnet written in disgust of vulgar superstition.*

The church bells toll a melancholy round,
Calling the people to some other prayers,
Some other gloominess, more dreadful cares,
More hearkening to the sermon's horrid sound.
Surely the mind of man is closely bound
In some black spell ; seeing that each one tears
Himself from fireside joys, and Lydian airs,
And converse high of those with glory crowned.
Still, still they toll, and I should feel a damp,—
A chill as from a tomb, did I not know
That they are dying like an outburnt lamp :
That 'tis their sighing, wailing ere they go
Into oblivion ;—that fresh flowers will grow
And many glories of immortal stamp.

JOHN KEATS.

Vraiment c'est bête, ces églises de villages,
Où quinze laids marmots encrassant les piliers,
Écoutent, grasseyant les divins babillages,
Un noir grotesque dont fermentent les souliers ;
Mais le soleil éveille, à travers les feuillages,
Les vieilles couleurs des vitraux irréguliers.

ARTHUR RIMBAUD.

Clericalism is still a danger—witness the fate of
unhappy Ireland ; therefore anti-clericalism is still a
duty. Vicariously, through the agency of Keats and
Rimbaud, I do my bit.

Keats's sonnet is not of the first order ; but it is at

least respectable and interesting. True, we must smile rather sadly at his assumption that all those who go to church are tearing themselves away ' from Lydian airs and converse high of those with glory crowned.'

In actual fact most of them are tearing themselves away from the murder cases and the football competitions of the Sunday Press. It is quite arguable that even the sermon's horrid sound is better than the drivel which men and women have left in order to hear it. But this does not, of course, excuse clericalism —does not relieve us from the duty of rooting it out in order to plant ' fresh flowers, and many glories of immortal stamp.'

As an attack on clericalism, the opening lines of Rimbaud's *Première Communion*, here quoted, are incomparably more effective than Keats's sonnet. 'Vraiment c'est bête, ces églises de villages ! ' This is exactly the right thing said in exactly the right tone. Keats lacked the gift of making the colloquial and the conversational take on the intensity of poetry. To make poetry out of his experience, he had, in his own words, to transform common Wellingtons into Romeo boots. Rimbaud could keep the Wellingtons and make them glow with mysterious fire. This piece of derisive anticlericalism is genuinely and beautifully poetic. And what admirable propaganda ! He makes us actually *smell* the priest's fermenting boots—ugh, with what unforgettable disgust !

# MONEY

As I sat in the café I said to myself,
They may talk as they please about what they call
    pelf,
They may sneer as they like about eating and
    drinking,
But help it I cannot, I cannot help thinking
    How pleasant it is to have money, heigh ho !
    How pleasant it is to have money.

I sit at my table *en grand seigneur*,
And when I have done, throw a crust to the poor ;
Not only the pleasure, one's self, of good living,
But also the pleasure of now and then giving.
    So pleasant it is to have money, heigh ho !
    So pleasant it is to have money.

I drive through the streets, and I care not a damn ;
The people they stare, and they ask who I am ;
And if I should chance to run over a cad,
I can pay for the damage, if ever so bad.
    So pleasant it is to have money, heigh ho !
    So pleasant it is to have money.

We stroll to our box and look down on the pit,
And if it weren't low should be tempted to spit ;
We loll and we talk until people look up,
And when it's half over, we go out to sup.
    So pleasant it is to have money, heigh ho !
    So pleasant it is to have money.

The best of the tables and the best of the fare—
And as for the others, the devil may care :

It isn't our fault if they dare not afford
To sup like a prince and be drunk as a lord.
    So pleasant it is to have money, heigh ho !
    So pleasant it is to have money.

They may talk as they please about what they call
    pelf
And how one ought never to think of one's self,
And how pleasures of thought surpass eating and
    drinking :—
My pleasure of thought is the pleasure of thinking
    How pleasant it is to have money, heigh ho !
    How pleasant it is to have money.
                       ARTHUR HUGH CLOUGH.


I have been in love, and in debt, and in drink,
    This many and many a year ;
And those three are plagues enough, one would think,
    For one poor mortal to bear.
'Twas drink made me fall into love,
    And love made me run into debt ;
And though I have struggled, and struggled, and
    strove,
    I cannot get out of them yet.

There's nothing but money can cure me,
    And rid me of all my pain ;
        'Twill pay all my debts
        And remove all my lets ;
And my mistress that cannot endure me,
    Will love me, and love me again :
Then I'll fall to loving and drinking again.
                       ALEXANDER BROME.

The part which money plays in the lives of even the least avaricious people is enormous. The part it plays in literature, and especially poetry, is very small. Moreover, poets seem to feel that money, if mentioned, has to be apologized for. This apology generally takes the form of a deprecatory touch of comedy. There is very little poetry in which economics are given what the Marxian theorists and the Fordian practitioners would certainly regard as their due.

This fact has a double explanation, social and psychological. Pagan philosophers and Christian theologians agreed in looking upon the love of money as evil ; while to the aristocracy, economic preoccupations seemed vulgar. The poet who wanted to write about money found himself hemmed in on every side ; he might not care much if people thought him wicked ; but vulgar—no, he could not run the risk of being considered that.

A Marxian would point out, quite justly, that this moral and aesthetic outlawing of economics was done by men who had an interest in the process. The pagan philosophers were members of a leisured class ; the Christian theologians had all their economic needs supplied by a great business organization, the aristocrats were what they were thanks to their wealth ; these people had no reason to discuss economics themselves and the very best reasons to prevent other people from asking awkward questions about their privileged position. Hence the taboo on money as a theme for literature. But this explanation, excellent so far as it goes, is not complete. There are internal as well as external reasons for the taboo, psychological as well as social reasons. Money is a peculiarly uninspiring theme. The distresses caused by its lack, though acute, are not of a kind which lend themselves to poetical treatment. Certain agonies are quickening and enlarging, have a natural tendency to break out into expression. Certain others, on the contrary, seem to numb the spirit and contract it. Economic miseries are essentially of the second class. Poets are not often moved to express this particular kind of emotion ; and when they try, they find that lyres are not tuned to give an adequate rendering of worry. The comic note is an apology, not only to society, but also to themselves ; they are apologizing to the critic within them for their own inability to do the job adequately.

Oft have I sung of Love and of his fire ;
But now I find that poet was advised,
Which made full feasts increasers of desire,
And proves weak Love was with the poor despised,
For when the life with food is not sufficed,
  What thoughts of love, what motion of delight,
  What pleasure can proceed from such a wight.
         ROBERT GREENE.

Greene is unromantically right. ' For,' in the appalling words of John Pomfret,

 . . . that which makes our life delightful prove
 Is a genteel sufficiency, and love—

and there can be no love without sufficiency, and none of the refinements of love, unless the sufficiency is at

174

least genteel. A reason, according to certain Marxian theorists, for disparaging love. For a thing which can exist only when there is a genteel sufficiency is bourgeois ; and what is bourgeois must be bad.

Now, the juxtaposition of, say, *Epipsychidion* and a bald account of the sources of Shelley's income would probably be rich in some very painful tragi-comic effects. ' He for love only, they (the peasantry on Sir Timothy Shelley's estates) for love in him.' It seems, certainly, rather an inequitable division of labour. But this injustice does nothing to lessen the value of the emotions expressed in *Epipsychidion*. Flowers are beautiful. But flowers, we discover, grow from dung. Must we therefore deny our immediate intuition and say that, after all, flowers are really ugly ? No ; if we are reasonable, we shall try to think of means for distributing dung to all potential gardeners, so that more flowers may be produced. Similarly we feel love to be a good ; a genteel sufficiency is the condition of love ; therefore, let us do our best to guarantee a genteel sufficiency to increasing numbers of human beings.


With her two brothers this fair lady dwelt,
   Enrichèd from ancestral merchandize,
And for them many a weary hand did swelt
   In torchèd mines and noisy factories,
And many once proud-quivered loins did melt
   In blood from stinging whip ; with hollow eyes
Many all day in dazzling river stood,
To take the rich-ored driftings of the flood.

For them the Ceylon diver held his breath,
    And went all naked to the hungry shark ;
For them his ears gushed blood ; for them in death
    The seal on the cold ice with piteous bark
Lay full of darts ; for them alone did seethe
    A thousand men in troubles wide and dark :
Half-ignorant, they turned an easy wheel,
That set sharp racks to work to pinch and peel.

JOHN KEATS.

Keats does for Isabella and her brothers the very thing which, as I suggested in an earlier paragraph, a Marxian critic of romantic values might do for the protagonists of *Epipsychidion*—he gives a description of their sumptuous and, in Isabella's case, emotionally refined existence, and follows it up with another (printed here) of the sources of that more than genteel sufficiency which made the luxury and refinement possible. The effect is good, but might have been very much better if Keats's artistic principles had allowed him for one moment to be 'unpoetical.' But, alas, they did not. Bare and brutal veracity is against his rules. He writes of sweated factory workers and the horrors of slavery in the same rather unreal, Wardour-Street language as he uses to describe mediaeval lords and ladies and the shepherds of Greek fable. The edge of his effect is thus blunted, the violence of what should have been the most startling of contrasts so muted and muffled that we hardly notice it, but read on, line after all-too-poetic line, soothed into a kind of hypnotic doze.

On Keats's, as on most of even the best nineteenth-century poetry, the curse of literariness lies heavy. How much better, on this economic theme, is Shelley, whose *Mask of Anarchy* contains perhaps the finest poetical account of economic slavery in the language. The best Marxian commentary on *Epipsychidion* has been written by the author of the poem himself.

> What is Freedom ?—ye can tell
> That which slavery is, too well—
> For its very name has grown
> To an echo of your own.
>
> 'Tis to work and have such pay
> As just keeps life from day to day
> In your limbs, as in a cell
> For the tyrant's use to dwell.
>
> So that ye for them are made
> Loom, and plough, and sword, and spàde,
> With or without your own will bent
> To their defence and nourishment.
>
> 'Tis to see your children weak
> With their mothers pine and peak,
> When the winter winds are bleak—
> They are dying, whilst I speak.
>
> 'Tis to hunger for such diet
> As the rich man in his riot
> Casts to the fat dogs that lie
> Surfeiting beneath his eye.
>
> 'Tis to be a slave in soul
> And to hold no strong control
> Over your own wills, but be
> All that others make of ye.

And at length, when ye complain
With a murmur weak and vain,
'Tis to see the Tyrant's crew
Ride over your wives and you—
Blood is on the grass like dew.

PERCY BYSSHE SHELLEY.

# HYPOCRISY

*(From the epilogue to ' Tartufe.' Spoken by Tartufe.)*

Zeal stands but sentry at the gate of sin,
Whilst all that have the word pass freely in :
Silent and in the dark, for fear of spies,
We march, and take Damnation by surprise ;
There's not a roaring blade in all this town
Can go so far towards Hell for half-a-crown
As I for sixpence, for I know the way.

CHARLES SACKVILLE, EARL OF DORSET.


## Le Châtiment de Tartufe

Tisonnant, tisonnant son cœur amoureux sous
Sa chaste robe noire, heureux, la main gantée,
Un jour qu'il s'en allait effroyablement doux,
Jaune, bavant la foi de sa bouche édentée,

Un jour qu'il s'en allait—' *Oremus* '—un méchant
Le prit rudement par son oreille benoîte
Et lui jeta des mots affreux, en arrachant
Sa chaste robe noire autour de sa peau moite.

Châtiment ! Ses habits étaient déboutonnés,
Et, le long chapelet des péchés pardonnés
S'égrenant dans son cœur, saint Tartufe était pâle.

Donc, il se confessait, priait, avec un râle.
L'homme se contenta d'emporter ses rabats.
—Peuh ! Tartufe était nu du haut jusques en bas.

ARTHUR RIMBAUD.

Sin, like art, is subject to the vagaries of fashion and

the fluctuations of taste. Moralists lay the emphasis now here, now there. Thus, in the ages of scarcity, gluttony ranked as a much deadlier sin than it does to-day, when we all ought to eat two or three times as much as we do, in order to keep down the surplus stocks of foodstuffs. Avarice, according to that Business Ethic, by which, for a hundred years past, most of the Western world has been forced to live, avarice is no longer a sin, but actually a virtue. Under the influence of socialist propaganda, it is now beginning to seem less creditable than it did a few years ago. Lechery, on the contrary, is going up in the ethical scale. The psychologists are busily engaged in making it individually respectable ; and at the same time the birth-controllers have robbed it of its unpleasant social consequences. The only sin which seems to us more sinful than it did to our fathers is cruelty. We feel for cruelty an abhorrence which would have seemed incomprehensible in the days of torture and public executions.

Next to acts of cruelty, lying is the offence that now appears to us most sinful—especially the long-drawn, elaborate lying which is hypocrisy. Tartufe is always with us, and we hate him at least as much as Molière hated him.

# THE WORST SIDE

Go, soul, the body's guest,
   Upon a thankless arrant ;
Fear not to touch the best,
   The truth shall be thy warrant :
Go, since I needs must die,
And give the world the lie.

Say to the Court, it glows
   And shines like rotten wood ;
Say to the Church, it shows
   What's good and doth no good :
If Church and Court reply,
Then give them both the lie.

Tell men of high condition,
   That manage the estate,
Their purpose is ambition,
   Their practice only hate :
And if they once reply,
Then give them all the lie.

Tell zeal it wants devotion,
   Tell love it is but lust,
Tell time it is but motion,
   Tell flesh it is but dust :
And wish them not reply,
For thou must give the lie.

So when thou hast, as I
   Commanded thee, done blabbing,
Although to give the lie
   Deserves no less than stabbing,

Stab at thee he that will ;
No stab the soul can kill.

SIR WALTER RALEIGH.

Ay, ay, *good man, kind father, best of friends*—
These are the words that grow, like grass and nettles,
Out of dead men, and speckled hatreds hide,
Like toads among them.

THOMAS LOVELL BEDDOES.

Birds feed on birds, beasts on each other prey ;
But savage man alone does man betray.
Pressed by necessity, they kill for food ;
Man undoes man to do himself no good.
With teeth and claws by nature armed, they hunt
Nature's allowance, to supply their want ;
But man with smiles, embraces, friendships, praise,
Unhumanly his fellow's life betrays,
With voluntary pains works his distress,
Not through necessity, but wantonness.
For hunger or for love they bite or tear,
Whilst wretched man is still in arms for fear ;
For fear he arms, and is of arms afraid,
From fear to fear successively betrayed.
Base fear, the source whence his best passion came,
His boasted honour and his dear-bought fame ;
That lust of power, to which he's such a slave,
And for the which alone he dares be brave ;
To which his various projects are designed,
Which make him generous, affable and kind.
Look to the bottom of his vast design,
Wherein man's wisdom, power and glory join,
The good he acts, the ill he does endure,
'Tis all for fear, to make himself secure.

Merely for safety after fame we thirst,
For all men would be cowards if they durst.
                JOHN WILMOT, EARL OF ROCHESTER.

My life is measured by this glass, this glass
By all those little sands that thorough pass.
See how they press, see how they strive, which shall
With greatest speed and greatest quickness fall.
See how they raise a little mount, and then
With their own weight do level it again.
But when they have all got thorough, they give o'er
Their nimble sliding down and move no more.
Just such is man, whose hours still forward run,
Being almost finished ere they are begun ;
So perfect nothings, such light blasts are we,
That ere we are aught at all, we cease to be.
Do what we will, our hasty minutes fly,
And while we sleep, what do we else but die ?
How transient are our joys, how short their day !
They creep on towards us, but fly away.
How stinging are our sorrows ! where they gain
But the least footing, there they will remain.
How groundless are our hopes, how they deceive
Our childish thoughts, and only sorrow leave !
How real are our fears ! they blast us still,
Still rend us, still with gnawing passions fill.
How senseless are our wishes, yet how great !
With what toil we pursue them, with what sweat !
Yet most times for our hurts, so small we see,
Like children crying for some mercury. . . .
Poor man, what art ?  A tennis ball of error,
A ship of glass tossed in a sea of terror,
Issuing in blood and sorrow from the womb,
Crawling in tears and mourning to the tomb ;

How slippery are thy paths, how sure thy fall,
How art thou nothing, when thou art most of all !

JOHN HALL.

Let him lean
Against his life, that glassy interval
'Twixt us and nothing ; and, upon the ground
Of his own slippery breath, draw hueless dreams,
And gaze on frost-work hopes.  Uncourteous Death
Knuckles the pane and . . .

THOMAS LOVELL BEDDOES.

# COMIC POETRY

What poor astronomers are they
   Take women's eyes for stars !
And set their thoughts in battle 'ray
   To fight such idle wars ;
When in the end they shall approve
'Tis but a jest drawn out of love.

And love itself is but a jest
   Devised by idle heads,
To catch young fancies in the nest
   And lay them in fools' beds ;
That being hatched in beauty's eyes,
They may be fledged ere they be wise.

But yet it is a sport to see
   How wit will run on wheels ;
While will cannot persuaded be
   With that which Reason feels,
That women's eyes and stars are odd
And love is but a feignèd god.

But such as will run mad with will
   I cannot clear their sight,
But leave them to their study still
   To look where is no light ;
Till—time too late—we make them try,
They study false astronomy.

ANON.

Ha ha ! ha ha ! this world doth pass
  Most merrily, I'll be sworn ;
For many an honest Indian ass
  Goes for an Unicorn.
       Farra diddle dino,
       This is idle fino.

Ty hye ! ty hye ! O sweet delight !
  He tickles this age that can
Call Tullia's ape a marmosite
  And Leda's goose a swan.
       Farra diddle dino,
       This is idle fino.

So so ! so so ! fine English days !
  When false play's no reproach ;
For he that doth the coachman praise
  May safely use the coach.
       Farra diddle dino,
       This is idle fino.

               ANON.

He that marries a merry lass,
  He has most cause to be sad :
For let her go free in her merry tricks,
  She'll work his patience mad.

But he that marries a scold, a scold,
He hath most cause to be merry ;
  For when she's in her fits
  He may cherish his wits
With singing, hey down derry !
He that weds a roaring girl
That will both scratch and fight,
  Though he study all day
  To make her away,
Will be glad to please her at night.

And he that copes with a sullen wench,
That scarce will speak at all,
  Her doggedness more
  Than a scold or a whore
Will penetrate his gall.

But he that's matched with a turtle dove
That hath no spleen about her
  Shall waste so much life
  In love of his wife,
He had better be without her.

ANON.

The Elizabethans had a secret, since irretrievably lost—the secret of being lyrically funny, of writing comic verses that are also beautiful. Here are three examples of this extinct loveliness. The first two are poetically the best. You could not ask for a prettier cadence than

    He tickles this age that can
    Call Tullia's ape a marmosite
    And Leda's goose a swan ;

or a livelier image than

    To catch young fancies in the nest
    And lay them in fools' beds.

But the third is also admirable. Admirable for the richness of its verbal flavour. (What grand locutions we have stupidly allowed to die ! ' Roaring girl,' for example, is a million times better than any equivalent since devised:) Admirable also in its substance. The poem is an abridged text-book of marriage.

To be a whore despite of grace,
Good council and an ugly face,
And to distribute still the pox
  To men of wit
Will seem a kind of paradox ;
  And yet
Thou art a whore, despite of grace,
Good council and an ugly face.

CHARLES COTTON.

When Orpheus went down to the regions below,
  Which men are forbidden to see,
He tuned up his lyre, as old histories show,
  To set his Eurydice free.

All hell was astonished a person so wise
  Should rashly endanger his life
And venture so far—but how vast their surprise,
  When they heard that he came for his wife !

To find out a punishment due to the fault
  Old Pluto had puzzled his brain ;
But hell had no torment sufficient, he thought—
  So he gave him his wife back again.

But pity succeeding found place in his heart
  And, pleased with his playing so well,
He took her again in reward of his art—
  Such merit had music in hell.

SAMUEL LISLE.

### Lot and his Daughters

    Il but,
  Il devint tendre ;
  Et puis il fut
    Son gendre.     ANON.

Compared with the best Elizabethan specimens, the comic poetry of later times seems, even when actually wittier and more amusing, rather poor stuff. Poor in not being beautiful. A certain natural and easy eloquence distinguished the comic verse of the Elizabethans, just as it distinguished their serious verse. Their fun is in the grand manner. Whereas ours is, and for the last two centuries has been, in the flippant manner—flippantly low, or else flippantly too high, mock-heroic. We make a radical distinction between the comic and the serious style. Which is a profound mistake. The best comic works have been grand and beautiful. Witness Rabelais and Aristophanes ; witness Daumier and our own magnificently and calligraphically grotesque Rowlandson. The Elizabethans used the same style (in their case a rich and musically flowing one) for both kinds of poetry. So did the Jacobeans and Carolines. These had two main styles for serious poetry—the ' witty,' ' metaphysical ' style and the colloquial style of everyday cultured speech. Both were employed very effectively in their comic verses. I quote a specimen of the second kind by Charles Cotton.

The flippant style came towards the end of the seventeenth century, and has remained the accredited style of comic poetry ever since. Its invention coincides with that of a special ' poetic diction ' for serious verse—of an artificial language remote from that of ordinary speech. Eighteenth - century diction went out of fashion about 1800—only to be replaced by another poetical argot, that of the Romantics, which is but now ceasing to be the official language of all serious verse. When this has finally gone the way of the conscious swains and finny tribes of an earlier dispensation, comic verse will get the chance of rising from its present Gilbertian degradation, up to that heaven of pure poetic beauty where Tullia's marmosite and Leda's goose have their supernatural being.

# CONCEITS

Yet once more, O ye laurels, and once more,
Ye myrtles brown, with ivy never sere,
I come to pluck your berries harsh and crude,
And with forced fingers rude
Shatter your leaves before the mellowing year. . . .

> I like not tears in tune, nor do I prize
> His artificial grief, who scans his eyes.
> Mine weep down pious beads ; but why should I
> Confine them to the muses' rosary ?
> I am no poet here ; my pen's the spout
> Where the rain-water of mine eyes runs out
> In pity of that name, whose fall we see
> Thus copied out in grief's hydrography. . . .

At the time of its publication, Cleveland's ode on the
death of Edward King was, I suspect, greatly preferred
in advanced literary circles to Milton's ; it must have
seemed so much more modern and on the spot. For an
intelligent undergraduate of the later sixteen-thirties,
phrases like ' grief's hydrography ' held, no doubt, that
quality of intense contemporariness which his successor
now finds, and feels to be so satisfactory, in almost any
of the imitations of 'Anna Livia Plurabelle.'

' Lycidas ' is one of the most staggering performances
in any literature ; having said which, I may admit that
I have a sneaking fondness for Cleveland. I like him
even when he is at his worst, as in this poem on Edward

King ; I like him for his very defects—for being so extraordinarily silly in his cleverness, for the really monstrous badness of his bad taste. I like him, also, for his merits. For he has merits. When he is good, he is very good. Thus, to a young lady, who had promised to be his mistress, but was dilatory in keeping her word, he could write :—

> Why does my she-advowson fly
> Incumbency ?

Which is a stroke of genius, a piece of the purest and most concentrated poetical utterance. Meaning is here under pressure, so to speak. There are only seven words ; but they carry the significance of seventy times seven. 'Advowson' suggests, by its sound, that Chaucerian offence of avouterie, so much resented by storks ; by its sense, the clergy—no better, the context implies, than they should be. The association clergy-adultery is always amusing and in the best poetical tradition. (' There is none other incubus but he.') As for ' incumbency '—it is a treàsure of etymological ambiguity. On the surface of the word we catch a glimpse of beneficed parsons settling down to porridge and sausages after morning prayers ; beneath, in the dimly-remembered, boyhood world of Latin grammar, flutter the literal meanings of *in* and *cubo*, with accompanying visions almost Pompeian in their unequivocalness.

A phrase of poetry drops into the mind like a stone into a pool. The waves go out and out in expanding circles. How soon will they break on a confining shore ? It depends on the native abilities and the acquired culture of each individual mind. A dull, uneducated spirit is a mere well, narrow between walls ; but in a lively and cultivated mind the waves can run on for the imaginative equivalent of miles and hours.

A good ' metaphysical ' conceit like this of Cleveland's is a poetical phrase of a peculiar and special kind. The waves it sets going are oddly shaped and have an eccentric motion. Instead of moving in regular circles across the mind, these waves will leave whole expanses of the pool unruffled, to come splashing up with a surprising and fantastic vehemence at one or two remote and unrelated points. The metaphysical poets always aimed at astonishing their readers, at compelling their attention by the association of the most unlikely ideas. The spectacle of strange bedfellows arbitrarily coupled is always absurd ; and so, in all such metaphysical conceits, there is a certain element of absurdity. When the poet knows his business, this is no defect ; the absurdity of a thing of beauty may actually heighten our pleasure in its beauty. When the poet does not know his business, the absurdity ruins everything. The association by Cleveland of grief with gutters is merely disastrous. The stone is dropped in the neighbourhood of death ; like a waterspout, the wave splashes up at the plumber's. It won't do. Whether another and a better poet might have made it do, I cannot guess. Probably not. Plumbing is, I suspect, too intrinsically Freudian and unspiritual ever to be satisfactorily associated with the nobler emotions.

One more paragraph by way of appendix. Shortly after writing this note on plumbing, I saw at Pommersfelden, in Franconia, a fifteenth-century painting, in which Cleveland's conceit is pictorially realized with all its implications. Christ is shown bleeding, and an angel collects the precious drops as they fall. But instead of collecting the blood directly from the wound, as angels always do in the paintings of the Italian primitives, this German angel collects it only when, in a positive torrent, it has run through an elaborate system of gutters and drain pipes, which discharge it, several feet below the platform on which the Saviour stands, through a large gilt spout. The picture illustrates only too well that disastrous tendency to over-emphasize and protest too much, which is the bane of all German art, from the Middle Ages to the present day. It also confirms all I have said about the incompatibility of plumbing with the higher feelings.

*Inscription on the tomb of Lady Mary Wentworth*

And here the precious dust is laid,
Whose purely tempered clay was made
So fine, that it the guest betrayed.

Else, the soul grew so fast within,
It broke the outward shell of sin,
And so was hatched a Cherubin.

In height it soared to God above,
In depth it did to knowledge move,
And spread in breadth to general love.

Good to the poor, to kindred dear,
To servants kind, to friendship clear,
To nothing but herself severe.

So, though a virgin, yet a bride
To every grace, she justified
A chaste polygamy, and died.

Learn from hence, reader, what small trust
We owe the world, where virtue must,
Frail as our flesh, crumble to dust.

THOMAS CAREW.

Death and plumbing cannot be coupled poetically. But death and polygamy can be. Carew has proved it.

So, though a virgin, yet a bride
To every grace, she justified
A chaste polygamy, and died.

It is absurd ; one is forced to smile. But at the same time one is touched, one does not forget the sadness of early death, one even believes in the lady's virtues. Smiling, one is yet charmed by the beauty of the verse, one admires the refined and delicate art with which the phrasing is managed. The absurdity of the metaphysical conceit does not take away from our aesthetic pleasure or neutralize our serious emotions ; it only changes their quality, gives them a new and peculiar flavour.

### Evening

The shadows now so long do grow
That brambles like tall cedars show ;
Molehills seem mountains, and the ant
Appears a monstrous elephant.
A very little, little flock
Shades thrice the ground that it would stock,

Whilst the small stripling following them
Appears a mighty Polypheme.

CHARLES COTTON.

### The Grasshopper : to Charles Cotton

O thou that swing'st upon the waving hair
   Of some well-fillèd oaten beard,
Drunk every night with a delicious tear
   Dropt thee from heaven, where thou wert reared !

The joys of earth and air are thine entire,
   That with thy feet and wings dost hop and fly ;
And when thy poppy works, thou dost retire
   To thy carved acorn-bed to lie.

Up with the day, the Sun thou welcomest then,
   Sport'st in the gilt plaits of his beams,
And all these merry days mak'st merry men,
   Thyself, and melancholy streams.

But, ah, the sickle ! golden ears are cropped ;
   Ceres and Bacchus bid good night ;
Sharp frosty fingers all your flowers have topped,
   And what scythes spared, winds shave off quite.

Poor verdant fool, and now green ice ! thy joys,
   Large and as lasting as thy perch of grass,
Bid us lay in 'gainst winter rain, and poise
   Their floods with an o'erflowing glass.

Thou best of men and friends ! we will create
   A genuine summer in each other's breast,
And spite of this cold time and frozen fate,
   Thaw us a warm seat to our rest.

RICHARD LOVELACE.

196

But now the salmon fishers moist
Their leathern boats begin to hoist
And, like antipodes in shoes,
Have shod their heads with their canoes.
How tortoise-like, but not so slow,
These rational amphibii go !
Let's in ; for the dark hemisphere
Does now like one of them appear.

ANDREW MARVELL.

Why should, of all things, man unruled
Such unproportioned dwellings build ?
The beasts are by their dens expressed,
And birds contrive an equal nest ;
The low-roofed tortoises do dwell
In cases fit of tortoise-shell :
No creature loves an empty space ;
Their bodies measure out their place.
But he, superfluously spread,
Demands more room alive than dead,
And in his hollow palace goes,
Where winds, as he, themselves may lose.
What need of all this marble crust
T' impark the wanton mote of dust ?

ANDREW MARVELL.

Dear Marvell's tortoises ! So absurd again—for the
tortoise is an intrinsically ridiculous animal ; but so
right where they are, so beautifully adapted, the one to
make us see the fishermen under their coracles and
night, hooded with its astronomical tent of shadow ;
the other to bring home the vanity of royal or pluto-

cratic magnificence.  Absurd, I repeat ;  but for that
very reason all the more poetical.


    Hope, whose weak being ruined is,
Alike if it succeed and if it miss ;
Whom good or ill does equally confound,
And both the horns of Fate's dilemma wound.
    Vain shadow, which does vanish quite
    Both at full noon and perfect night !
The stars have not a possibility
    Of blessing thee ;
If things then from their end we happy call,
'Tis hope is the most hopeless thing of all.

    Hope, thou bold taster of delight,
Who, whilst thou shouldst but taste, devour'st it
    quite !
Thou bring'st us an estate, yet leav'st us poor
By clogging it with legacies before.
    The joys which we entire should wed
    Come deflowered virgins to our bed ;
Good fortunes without gain imported be,
    Such mighty custom's paid to thee.
For joy, like wine, kept close does better taste ;
If it take air before, its spirits waste.

    Hope, fortune's cheating lottery,
Where for one prize a hundred blanks there be !
Fond archer, Hope, who tak'st thy aim so far,
That still or short or wide thine arrows are !
    Thin, empty cloud, which the eye deceives
With shapes that our own fancy gives !
A cloud which gilt and painted now appears,
    But must drop presently in tears !

When thy false beams o'er reason's light prevail,
By *ignes fatui* for North Stars we sail.

Brother of fear, more gaily clad !
The merrier fool o' the two, yet quite as mad !
Sire of repentance, child of fond desire,
That blow'st the Chymic's and the Lover's fire !
  Leading them still insensibly on
  By the strange witchcraft of *Anon* !
By thee the one does changing Nature through
Her endless labyrinths pursue,
And the other chases woman, whilst she goes
More ways and turns than hunted Nature knows.

ABRAHAM COWLEY.


### Upon Nothing

Nothing, thou elder brother even to shade,
Thou hadst a being ere the world was made
And, well fixed, art of ending not afraid.

Ere time and place were, time and place were not,
When primitive nothing something straight begot ;
Then all proceeded from the great united ' what ? '

Something, the general attribute of all,
Severed from thee, its sole original,
Into thy boundless self must undistinguished fall.

Yet something did thy mighty power command,
And from thy fruitful emptiness's hand
Snatch men, beasts, birds, fire, water, air and
    land. . . .

But, nothing, why does something still permit
That sacred monarchs should at council sit
With persons highly thought, at best for nothing fit ?

199

While weighty something modestly abstains
From prince's coffers  and from statesmen's brains,
And nothing there like stately nothing reigns.

JOHN WILMOT, EARL OF ROCHESTER.

Irrelevances brought startlingly, and herefore absurdly, together are the stuff of most metaphysical conceits.  But the seventeenth-century poets also employed another device for making the reader ' sit up.' Instead of ranging over heaven and earth for an unlikely similitude to the object under consideration, they sometimes turned a fixed and penetrating gaze upon the object itself.  This microscopic examination revealed various qualities inherent in the object, but not apparent to the superficial glance.  The essence of the thing was, so to speak, brought to the surface and revealed itself as being no less remote from, no less irrelevant to, the conception framed by common sense than the most far-fetched analogy.

Thus, Rochester's analysis ingeniously shows that nothing is so unlike a thing as the thing itself.  The thing, in this particular case, is Nothing ; nothing is so unlike Nothing as Nothing.  The coupling of Nothing, philosophically considered, with the everyday Nothing of common sense produces the most startling effects. Nothing proves itself to be quite as absurdly irrelevant to Nothing as gutters are to grief, or as tortoises to grandeur.  The writer who exploited this kind of metaphysical conceit most thoroughly and most ingeniously was Lewis Carroll.  Born two hundred years earlier, he would have left behind him, not a children's book but a long devotional poem in the style of Benlowes.

# COLLOQUIALISM AND THE POETRY OF COMMON LIFE

> Go, Mary, to the summer house
> And sweep the wooden floor,
> And light the little fire, and wash
> The pretty varnished door ;
> For there the London gentleman,
> Who lately lectured here,
> Will smoke a pipe with Jonathan,
> And taste our home-brewed beer.
>
> Go bind the dahlias, that our guest
> May praise their fading dyes ;
> But strip of every fading bloom
> The flower that won the prize !
> And take thy father's knife, and prune
> The roses that remain,
> And let the fallen hollyhock
> Peep through the broken pane.
>
> I'll follow in an hour or two ;
> Be sure I will not fail
> To bring his flute and spying glass,
> The pipes and bottled ale ;
> And that grand music that he made
> About the child in bliss,
> Our guest shall hear it sung and played,
> And feel how grand it is !
>
> EBENEZER ELLIOTT.

What is the secret of the peculiar repulsiveness of these verses ? (For repulsive they are, almost mystically and transcendentally so.) It is to be found, I think, in

their author's complacent acquiescence in the commonness of common life—in the commonness that is
common and unclean, rather than common and sublime, or at the least decent.

The Corn Law Rhymer's deserving poors are disgustingly conscious of being deserving ; worse, they are
vain of their deservingness.  They long to show off
before the London gentleman, to display their prize
dahlia and their culture, their pretty varnished door
and even (revolting exhibitionism !) their feelings
about the dead child—such nice genteel feelings, expressed in terms of music that even a London gentleman must feel to be grand ! To ask us, as the good
Ebenezer does, to take such commonness seriously,
with a tear in the eye and a pious snuffle in the nose, is
an outrage. 'How I loathe ordinariness !' (The
words are Lawrence's.)  'How from my soul I abhor
nice simple people, with their eternal price list !  It
makes my blood boil.' The proper style in which to
write about that sort of common life is the style adopted
by Laurent Tailhade in the *Poèmes Aristophanesques*.

Ce qui fait que l'ancien bandagiste renie
Le comptoir dont le faste alléchait les passants,
C'est son jardin d'Auteuil où, veufs de tout encens,
Les zinnias ont l'air d'être en tôle vernie.

C'est là qu'il vient le soir, goûter l'air aromal
Et, dans sa *rocking chair*, en veston de flanelle,
Aspirer les senteurs qu'épanchent sur Grenelle
Les fabriques de suif et de noir animal.

Bien que libre-penseur et franc-maçon, il juge
Le dieu propice qui lui donna ce refuge
202

Où se meurt un cyprin emmy la pièce d'eau,
Où, dans la tour mauresque aux lanternes chinoises,
—Tout en lui préparant du sirop de framboises,—
Sa ' demoiselle ' chante un couplet de Nadaud.

The retired rubber-goods merchant, it will be noticed, is celebrated in a sonnet and in the most elaborately poetical language. Homeliness and colloquialism are the weapons best fitted to puncture an intellectual or spiritual pretentiousness. Common uncleanness is best combated with an uncommon refinement of far-fetched language. Hence the mock heroic style. Satire does most of its killing by allopathy. To deal really adequately with Ebenezer's deserving poors one would have to use polysyllables and the manner of *Paradise Lost*.

To the common and unclean our reaction is negative, a revulsion ; to the common and decent, on the conrary, it is joyfully positive. To treat the common decencies colloquially, which is to treat them on the common plane, seems therefore natural and right. Colloquialism testifies to the poet's complete and unreserved acceptance of his subject.

The poet who would write of common things in common, colloquial language is beset with two great difficulties. To begin with, he must make his colloquialism genuinely colloquial—' a selection,' in Wordsworth's words, ' of the real language of men in a state of vivid sensation,' a dialect actually spoken, or at any rate speakable, by some class of genuine human beings. Poems like ' The Idiot Boy ' are unsatisfactory because, among other reasons, Wordsworth did not

use the language really used by men.  He tried to be
colloquial and failed.

> And Betty's husband's at the wood,
> Where by the week he doth abide,
> A woodman in the distant vale :—

This is not the language actually spoken by human
beings.  It is bad poetic diction.  Wordsworth could
never strip off the last clinging rags of linguistic fancy
dress.  Hence his failure to write good colloquial
poetry ;  and hence the failure of so many others who
have tried to do what he essayed in the Lyrical Ballads.
The other difficulty confronting the colloquial poet is
the difficulty of giving to colloquialisms the sharpness
and the memorable concentration required of poetic
language.  Thus, ' The Idiot Boy,' when it *is* colloquial
and not conventionally poetic, is diffuse and dim in its
colloquialism.  But colloquialism, as the following
example proves, need not be dim.

> Depuis huit jours, j'avais déchiré mes bottines
> Aux cailloux des chemins ; j'entrais à Charleroi.
> Au *Cabaret Vert* je demandais des tartines
> De beurre et du jambon qui fût a moitié froid.

> Bienheureux j'allongeais les jambes sous la table
> Verte ; je contemplais les sujets très naïfs
> De la tapisserie.  Et ce fut adorable,
> Quand la fille aux tétons énormes, aux yeux vifs,

> —Celle-là, ce n'est pas un baiser qui l'épeure !—
> Rieuse, m'apporta des tartines de beurre,
> Du jambon tiède dans un plat colorié.

204

COLLOQUIALISMS

Du jambon rose et blanc parfumé d'une gousse
D'ail et m'emplit la chope immense avec sa mousse
Que dorait un rayon de soleil arriéré.

ARTHUR RIMBAUD.

If only Wordsworth could ever have written something like this ! But, alas, whatever feelings he may once have had for beer and bosomy barmaids and the pink and white internal complexion of ham were early stifled. And Rimbaud's infallible ear, that he never possessed. Those delicate rhythmical effects by means of which the boy poet heightened his colloquialisms to the pitch of lyrical intensity were quite beyond Wordsworth. Indeed, so far from heightening colloquial speech, Wordsworth often contrived, in the process of 'fitting a metrical arrangement,' actually to lower it.

> Poor Susan moans, poor Susan groans ;
> The clock gives warning for eleven ;
> 'Tis on the stroke—' He must be near,'
> Quoth Betty, ' and will soon be here,
> As sure as there's a moon in heaven.'

> The clock is on the stroke of twelve,
> And Johnny is not yet in sight :
> The Moon's in heaven, as Betty sees,
> But Betty is not quite at ease ;
> And Susan has a dreadful night.

Almost any old countrywoman's account of these events would be much sharper, much more penetratingly intense than this. Wordsworth's versifying has had the effect of taking the bright edge off ' the real language of men in a state of vivid sensation.'

## Two Sisters

### I

Alice is tall and upright as a pine,
White as blanched almonds or the falling snow,
Sweet as are damask roses when they blow,
And doubtless fruitful as the swelling vine.
Ripe to be cut and ready to be pressed,
Her full-cheeked beauties very well appear,
And a year's fruit she loses every year,
Wanting a man to improve her to the best.
Full fain she would be husbanded, and yet,
Alas, she cannot a fit labourer get
To cultivate her to his own content :
Fain would she be, God wot, about her task,
And yet, forsooth, she is too proud to ask,
And (which is worse) too modest to consent.

### II

Margaret of humbler stature by the head
Is (as it oft falls out with yellow hair)
Than her fair sister, yet so much more fair
As her pure white is better mixt with red.
This, hotter than the other ten to one,
Longs to be put unto her mother's trade,
And loud proclaims she lives too long a maid,
Wishing for one to untie her virgin zone.
She finds virginity a kind of ware
That's very, very troublesome to bear,
And being gone she thinks will ne'er be missed ;
And yet withal the girl has so much grace,
To call for help I know she wants the face,
Though, asked, I know not how she would resist.

CHARLES COTTON.

Apart from Milton, almost all the good poets of the seventeenth century are colloquial poets ; they write a language spoken or speakable by any cultivated gentleman. Herbert is gravely colloquial about God ; Herrick, gaily, about girls and flowers. All are talkers.

In these two sonnets by Charles Cotton the talk is particularly light, humorous and easy. Reading, we seem to hear a warm and cultured voice discoursing across the dinner table. It is delightful—all the more so since this knowledgeable chat about feminine charms and feminine temperaments is also genuinely poetry.

For the poetical heightening of his speech, Cotton relies, partly on rhythm, partly on a judicious choice of images. How admirably phrased, for example, is the first quatrain of the second sonnet ! Curiously stretched, the syntax seems to vibrate under the impact of the meaning ; a simple conversational statement goes out, in consequence, with a peculiar and unexpected reson-ance. And how apposite, with its suggestion of some-thing good to eat—*de délicieux à croquer*—is ' white as blanched almonds' ! And at the sound of ' full-cheeked beauties' what a vision swims up before the inward eye! Peonies, peaches, the backsides of cherubs, a whole Wallace Collection of Bouchers and Fragonards. . . .

> Some people hang portraits up
> In a room where they dine or sup :
> And the wife clinks tea-things under,
> And her cousin, he stirs his cup,
> Asks, ' who was the lady, I wonder ? '
> ' 'Tis a daub John bought at a sale,'
> Quoth the wife—looks black as thunder :

' What a shade beneath her nose !
Snuff-taking, I suppose,'
Adds the cousin, while John's corns ail.
Or else there's no wife in the case,
But the portrait's Queen of the place,
Alone 'mid the other spoils
Of youth—masks, gloves and foils,
And pipe-sticks, rose, cherry-tree, jasmine,
And the long whip, the tandem-lasher,
And the cast of a fist (' not alas mine,
But my master's, the Tipton Slasher '),
And the cards where pistol-balls mark ace,
And a satin shoe used for cigar-case,
And the chamois horns (' shot in the Chablais '),
And prints—Rarey drumming on Cruiser,
And Sayers, our champion, the bruiser,
And the little edition of Rabelais :
Where a friend, with both hands in his pockets,
May saunter up close to examine it,
And remark a good deal of Jane Lamb in it,
' But the eyes are half out of their sockets :
That hair's not so bad, where the gloss is,
But they've made the girl's nose a proboscis :
Jane Lamb, that we danced with at Vichy !
What, isn't she Jane ?  Then, who is she ? '

All that I own is a print,
An etching, a mezzotint ;
'Tis a study, a fancy, a fiction,
Yet a fact (take my conviction)
Because it has more than a hint
Of a certain face, I never
Saw elsewhere touch or trace of
In women I've seen the face of :

Just an etching, and, so far, clever.

I keep my prints, an imbroglio,
Fifty in one portfolio.
When somebody tries my claret,
We turn round chairs to the fire,
Chirp over days in a garret,
Chuckle o'er increase in salary,
Taste the good fruits of our leisure,
Talk about pencil and lyre,
And the National Portrait Gallery :
Then I exhibit my treasure.
After we've turned over twenty,
And the debt of wonder my crony owes
Is paid to my Marc Antonios,
He stops me—' *Festina lente !*
What's that sweet thing there, the etching ? '
How my waistcoat strings want stretching,
How my cheeks grow red as tomatoes,
How my heart leaps ! But hearts, after leaps, ache.

' By the by, you must take, for a keepsake,
That other, you praised, of Volpato's.'
The fool ! Would he try a flight further and say—
He never saw, never before to-day,
What was able to take his breath away,
A face to lose youth for, to occupy age
With the dream of, meet death with,—why, I'll not
    engage
But that, half in a rapture and half in a rage,
I should toss him the thing's self—' 'Tis only a
    duplicate,
A thing of no value ! Take it, I supplicate ! '

ROBERT BROWNING.

What is he buzzing in my ears ?
  ' Now that I come to die,
Do I view the world as a vale of tears ? '
  Ah, reverend sir, not I !

What I viewed there once, what I view again
  Where the physic bottles stand
On the table's edge,—is a suburb lane,
  With a wall to my bedside hand.

That lane sloped, much as the bottles do,
  From a house you could descry
O'er the garden wall : is the curtain blue
  Or green to a healthy eye ?

To mine, it serves for the old June weather
  Blue above lane and wall :
And that furthest bottle labelled ' Ether '
  Is the house o'ertopping all.

At a terrace, somewhere near the stopper,
  There watched for me, one June,
A girl : I know, sir, it's improper,
  My poor mind's out of tune.

Only, there was a way . . . you crept
  Close by the side, to dodge
Eyes in the house, two eyes except :
  They styled their house ' The Lodge.'

What right had a lounger up their lane ?
  But, by creeping very close,
With the good wall's help, their eyes might strain
  And stretch themselves to Oos,

Yet never catch her and me together,
  As she left the attic, there,

By the rim of the bottle labelled ' Ether,'
  And stole from stair to stair.

And stood by the rose-wreathed gate.   Alas,
  We loved, sir—used to meet :
How sad and bad and mad it was—
  But then, how it was sweet !

ROBERT BROWNING.

# DESCRIPTIONS

Ante fores tumuli, quas saxa immania duro
obice dampnarant, scopulis substructa cavatis,
stat Dominus, nomenque ciet frigentis amici.
Nec mora, funereus revolutis rupibus horror
evomit exsequias gradiente cadavere vivas.
Solvite jam lætæ redolentia vincla sorores.
Solus odor sparsi spiramen aromatis efflat,
nec de corporeo nidorem sordida tabo
aura refert, oculos sanie stillante solutos
pristinus in speculum decor excitat, et putrefactas
tincta rubore genas paulatim purpura vestit.
Quis potuit fluidis animam suffundere membris ?
Nimirum qui membra dedit, qui fictilis ulvæ
perflavit venam madidam, cui tabida gleba
traxit sanguineos infecto humore colores.

PRUDENTIUS.

A description so scientifically accurate, so fully
realized in all its details, as this of the gradually de-
putrefying Lazarus, is positively alarming. Reading
such passages (and they seem to be fairly common in
later Latin poetry) one realizes how extremely unprecise most of the best poetical descriptions are.
Poets are seldom much interested in the precise look
of things ; they are interested in the mind's reaction to
the things. This reaction can generally be rendered
quite effectively without resorting to precise description. Indeed, precise description often hinders the
poet in his task of expressing what the things have
caused him to feel.

La très-chère était nue, et connaissant mon cœur,
Elle n'avait gardé que ses bijoux sonores,
Dont le riche attirail lui donnait l'air vainqueur
Qu'ont dans leurs jours heureux les esclaves des
      Maures.

Quand il jette en dansant son bruit vif et moqueur,
Ce monde rayonnant de métal et de pierre
Me ravit en extase, et j'aime avec fureur
Les choses où le son se mêle à la lumière.

Elle était donc couchée, et se laissait aimer,
Et du haut du divan elle souriait d'aise
A mon amour profond et doux comme la mer
Qui vers elle montait comme vers sa falaise.

Les yeux fixés sur moi, comme un tigre dompté,
D'un air vague et rêveur, elle essayait des poses,
Et la candeur unie à la lubricité
Donnait un charme neuf à ses métamorphoses.

Et son bras et sa jambe, et sa cuisse et ses reins,
Polis comme de l'huile, onduleux comme un cygne,
Passaient devant mes yeux clairvoyants et sereins ;
Et son ventre et ses seins, ces grappes de ma vigne.

Je croyais voir unis par un nouveau dessin
Les hanches de l'Antiope au buste d'un imberbe,
Tant sa taille faisait ressortir son bassin ;
Sur ce teint fauve et brun le fard était superbe !

Et la lampe s'étant résignée à mourir,
Comme le foyer seul illuminait la chambre,
Chaque fois qu'il poussait un flamboyant soupir,
Il inondait de sang cette peau couleur d'ambre !

CHARLES BAUDELAIRE.

With an equal precision, Baudelaire describes both
what is seen and the feeling of the seer.  Realized with
extraordinary pictorial intensity, the naked mulatto
woman lies there before us ;  and our eyes, as we read,
become those of the poet in his strange ecstasy of de-
tached, intellectual, platonic sensuality.


In the worst inn's worst room, with mat half hung,
The floor of plaster and the walls of dung,
On once a flock-bed, but repaired with straw,
With tape-tied curtains, never meant to draw,
The George and Garter dangling from that bed,
Where tawdry yellow strove with dirty red,
Great Villiers lies—alas, how changed from him,
That life of pleasure, and that soul of whim !
Gallant and gay in Clivedon's proud alcove,
The bower of wanton Shrewsbury and love :
Or just as gay, at council, in the ring
Of mimic statesmen, and their merry king.
No wit to flatter, left of all his store !
No fool to laugh at, which he valued more.
There, victor of his health, of fortune, friends,
And fame, this lord of useless thousands ends.

ALEXANDER POPE.

The theorists of ' Classicism ' decreed that all
poetical descriptions should be couched in general
terms.  In spite of which, this admirable purple passage
from the Epistle to Lord Bathurst is full of the most
accurate particularities.

I remember, the first time I read Pope's lines, being
profoundly impressed by those walls of dung.  Indeed,

they still disturb my imagination. They express, for me, the Essential Horror. A floor of dung would have seemed almost normal, acceptable. But *walls*—Ah, no, no !

His body was as straight as Circe's wand ;
Jove might have sipped out nectar from his hand.
Even as delicious meat is to the taste,
So was his neck in touching, and surpassed
The white of Pelops' shoulder : I could tell ye
How smooth his breast was and how white his belly ;
And whose immortal fingers did imprint
That heavenly path with many a curious dint
That runs along his back ; but my rude pen
Can hardly blazon forth the loves of men,
Much less of powerful gods.

CHRISTOPHER MARLOWE.

This was the loveliest boy that ever lived. Of the fact of his beauty Marlowe's description convinces us beyond the possibility of doubt. And yet how little he actually says about the boy ! And how indefinite, vague and unspecified is all that he does say ! There is, in actual fact, no description at all. Marlowe simply catalogues parts of the boy's body in association with certain names from classical mythology. The effect is extraordinary : we see the divine creature and instantly fall in love with him.

Fair is my love that feeds among the lilies,
The lilies growing in that pleasant garden,
Where cupid's mount, that well-beloved hill is,
And where the little god himself is warden.

See where my love sits in the bed of spices,
Beset all round with camphor, myrrh and roses,
And interlaced with curious devices,
Which her from all the world apart incloses.

BARTHOLOMEW GRIFFIN.

There is no description here ; but the lady's beauty
and attractiveness are none the less effectively rendered
by implication.   There is, to begin with, the versification—how luscious in its melodiousness !  The lady, to
whom these lines refer, must be as sleekly undulous as
they.   In the next place, she lives among lilies, in a
pleasant garden, on a mount that is Cupid's, bedded in
spicery.   All these are images highly agreeable in themselves and further significant in being, quite frankly and
manifestly, sexual symbols.   Often the best way of
expressing the nature of one thing is by talking about
another.

But, might we her sweet breast, Love's Eden, see :
    On those snow mountlets apples be,
May cure those mischiefs wrought by the forbidden
    tree.

Her hands are soft as swanny down, and much
    More white ;  whose temperate warmth is such,
As when ripe gold and quickening sunbeams inly
    touch.

Ye sirens of the groves, who, perched on high,
    Tune guttural sweets, air-ministrels, why
From your bough-cradles, rocked with wind, to her
    d'ye fly ?

Thou art silver-voiced, teeth-pearled, thy head's gold-
    thatched ;
  Nature's reviver, Flora's patched
(Though tricked in May's new raiment) when with
    thee she's matched.

EDWARD BENLOWES.

I serve a mistress whiter than the snow,
  Straighter than cedar, brighter than the glass,
Finer in trip and swifter than the roe,
  More pleasant than the field of flowering grass ;
More gladsome to my withering hopes that fade
Than winter's sun, or summer's cooling shade.

Sweeter than swelling grape of ripest wine,
  Softer than feathers of the fairest swan,
Smoother than jet, more stately than the pine,
  Fresher than poplar, smaller than my span,
Clearer than beauty's fiery-pointed beam,
Or icy crust of crystal's frozen stream.

Yet is she curster than the bear by kind,
  And harder hearted than the aged oak,
More glib than oil, more fickle than the wind,
  Stiffer than steel, no sooner bent but broke.
Lo thus my service is a lasting sore ;
Yet will I serve, although I die therefore.

ANTHONY MUNDAY.

# NONSENSE

Come on, ye critics, find one fault who dares ;
For read it backwards, like a witch's prayers,
'Twill read as well ; throw not away your jests
On solid nonsense that abides all tests.
Wit, like tierce-claret, when 't begin to pall,
Neglected lies and 's of no use at all ;
But, in its full perfection of decay,
Turns vinegar, and comes again in play. . . .
As skilful divers to the bottom fall
Sooner than those who cannot swim at all,
So, in this way of writing without thinking,
Thou hast a strange alacrity in sinking.
Thou writ'st below even thy own natural parts,
And with acquired dullness and new arts
Of studied nonsense tak'st kind readers' hearts.

CHARLES SACKVILLE, EARL OF DORSET.

It was a famous anecdote about the author of these
lines that called forth from Dr. Johnson one of his most
admirably Johnsonian, one, also, of his most depressing remarks. ' On the night before the battle, he is
said to have composed the celebrated song, " To all
you Ladies now on Land," with equal tranquillity of
mind and promptitude of wit. *Seldom any splendid story
is wholly true.* I have heard from the late Earl of
Orrery that Lord Buckhurst had been employed a week
upon it.'

Dorset's conception of an artistic badness so extreme
that it comes round, full circle—or, rather, full spiral—
and turns into a kind of goodness on another plane, is

218

subtle and profound. It serves to explain our delight in such works as ' Irene Iddesleigh,' and why we like the *papier mâché* furniture of 1850.

# OBSCURITY IN POETRY

Who says that fiction only and false hair
Become a verse ? Is there in truth no beauty ?
Is all good structure in a winding stair ?
May no lines pass, except they do their duty
   Not to a true, but painted chair ?

Is it no verse, except enchanted groves
And sudden arbours shadow coarse-spun lines ?
Must purling streams refresh a lover's loves ?
Must all be veiled, while he that reads divines,
   Catching the sense at two removes ?

GEORGE HERBERT.

Across three centuries George Herbert's questions
address themselves (how pertinently !) to us.

Obscurity in poetry is by no means always to be
avoided. Shakespeare, for example, is one of the most
difficult of authors. He often writes obscurely, for the
good reason that he often has subtle and uncommon
thoughts to put into words. So have some of the poets
writing obscurely at the present time. Most, however,
have not. Their thoughts and the way they see the
world, are commonplace ; only their syntax is extraordinary. Almost all the contents of the ' advanced '
reviews are just ' Mary had a little lamb ' translated
into Hebrew and written in cipher. Re-Englished and
decoded, they astonish the reader by their silliness.
Catching the sense at two removes, or ten, he is
annoyed to find that it is either nonsense or platitude.

# MAGIC

Trinitas, deitas, unitas æterna,
Majestas, potestas, pietas superna.
Sol, lumen et numen, cacumen, semita,
Lapis, mons, petra, fons, flumen, pons et vita.
Tu sator, creator, amator, redemptor, salvator,
    luxque perpetua,
Tu tutor et decor, tu candor, tu splendor et odor quo
    vivunt mortua.
Tu vertex et apex, regum rex, legum lex et vindex,
    tu lux angelica,
Quem clamant, adorant, quem laudant, quem
    cantant, quem amant agmina cœlica.
Tu theos et heros, dives flos, vivens ros, rege nos,
    salva nos, perduc nos ad thronos superos et vera
    gaudia.
Tu decus et virtus, tu justus et verus, tu sanctus et
    bonus, tu rectus et summus Dominus, tibi sit
    gloria.

PIERRE DE CORBEIL.

Amara tanta tyri pastos sycalos sycalire
cellivoli scarras polili posylique lyvarras.

MAGIC SPELL, 12TH CENTURY.

Horse and hattock,
Horse and go,
Horse and pelatis, Ho, ho !

SPELL USED BY WITCHES WHEN
MOUNTING THEIR BROOMSTICKS.

ἔριφος ἐς γάλ᾽ ἔπετον
(A kid, I fell into milk.)

ORPHIC FORMULA.

Intrinsically magical, spells are loud with what is, for us, a compelling music. Their phrases are thrillingly obscure with shadowed meanings and mysterious allusions. Their strange words set the imagination working. Spells, in short, are poetry, and their authors, the magicians, poets. The thing is psychologically inevitable. If words had not first moved him, how could man have come to believe that they would move things ? And is it likely that he would set out to move things by means of incantations which left him unmoved ? But words which move are poetry. Magicians, I repeat, are always poets.

Poetry justifies belief in magic. In an anthropomorphic world belief in the efficacity of abracadabra is imposed by simple logic. ' I know by experience that words have power over me. The external world is, by definition, of the same nature as myself. Therefore words must have power over the external world.' The syllogism is unanswerably sound. Only when we have ceased to believe that the macrocosm is a large-scale model of ourselves, does the argument lose its force. To-day we know, at any rate in our more rational moments, that magic is effective only on ourselves. We employ spells to move, not matter, but our own emotions.

All literature is a mixture, in varying proportions, of magic and science. Text-books are almost unadulteratedly scientific. (I say ' almost ' advisedly.

222

For text-books are not all alike. Some are thoroughly legible. Others do not permit themselves to be read. The legible ones are those whose authors have contrived to introduce into their exposition a leavening of magic. They have known how to combine words in such a way that the phrases penetrate the understanding and remain there, rumbling with a memorable noise.) At the other end of the scale we find writings like Joyce's ' Anna Livia Plurabelle,' or like Nashe's ' Have with you to Saffron Walden,' or like some of the later poems of Mallarmé, or like certain passages in Sterne and Virginia Woolf—writings in which the principal, sometimes almost the sole, ingredient is magic. The great bulk of literature is a compromise lying between the two extremes.

    (*A Head comes up with ears of corn, and she combs them into her lap.*)
Gently dip, but not too deep,
For fear you make the golden beard to weep.
Fair maiden, white and red,
Comb me smooth and stroke my head,
And thou shalt have some cockell-bread.

    (*A second Head comes up full of gold, which she combs into her lap.*)
Gently dip, but not too deep,
For fear thou make the golden beard to weep.
Fair maid, white and red,
Comb me smooth and stroke my head,
And every hair a sheaf shall be,
And every sheaf a golden tree.    GEORGE PEELE.

Magicians are always poets, but not always very good poets. Professionals can generally improve upon their workmanship. Witness this lovely spell from ' The Old Wives Tale.' Peele is the master of most excellent Elizabethan sound-magic and past-master of what I may call that ' magic of irrelevance,' which is produced by the introduction into one context of ideas and images which seem to belong to another. Thus, the golden beard weeps. The reward for combing the hair is to be (for no apparent reason) some cockell bread—a substance whose most curious mode of manufacture is described by John Aubrey. Finally, every hair is to be a sheaf and every sheaf a golden tree. Though not a spell, the song and soliloquy with which the same author's ' David and Bethsabe ' opens is no less magical, and with a similar magic.

*Bethsabe, bathing, sings, then speaks :*

Hot sun, cool fire, tempered with sweet air,
Black shade, fair nurse, shadow my white hair ;
Shine, sun ; burn, fire ; breathe, air, and ease me ;
Black shade, fair nurse, shroud me and please me ;
Shadow, my sweet nurse, keep me from burning,
Make not my glad cause cause of mourning.
   Let not my beauty's fire
   Inflame unstaid desire,
   Nor pierce any bright eye
   That wandereth lightly.

Come, gentle Zephyr, trickt with those perfumes
That erst in Eden sweetened Adam's love,
And stroke my body with thy silken fan.

This shade, sun proof, is yet no proof for thee ;
Thy body smoother than this waveless spring
And purer than the substance of the same,
Can creep through that *his* lances cannot pierce.

GEORGE PEELE.

The sound here is manifestly supernatural. (Did not Mohammed adduce the beauty of his style as an argument for the divine inspiration of the Koran ?) And with what subtle recklessness do the irrelevances succeed one another in ' black shade, fair nurse, shadow my white hair ' ; in ' black shade, fair nurse, shroud me and please me ' ! The magic of irrelevance is one of poetry's most powerful instruments. Why are poetical phrases poetical ? In most cases, because they contain ideas which we normally regard as irrelevant one to another, but which the poet has contrived to make relevant. ' Sleep that knits up the ravelled sleave of care ' ; ' to the last syllable of recorded time ' ; ' those milk paps that through the window bars bore at men's eyes.' Embroidery and misery ; time and spelling ; breasts and gimlets—Shakespeare's plays are a tissue of such odd, but, as he uses them, profoundly significant irrelevances. Every good metaphor is the mating of irrelevances to produce a new and more vivid expression.

But sometimes, as in the two songs by Peele, quoted above, irrelevance is used with a kind of recklessness, for its own sake, so to speak. Milk paps through the window bars bore at men's eyes in order that the idea of physical desire may be expressed with a new and peculiar intensity. But weeping and the golden beard,

225

combing and cockell bread, hair and sheaves, and sheaves and trees—these are brought together simply in order to produce an effect of strangeness. 'The woods decay,' writes Tennyson,

> the woods decay and fall,
> The vapours weep their burden to the ground.
> Man comes and tills the field and lies beneath,
> And after many a summer dies the swan.

Why the swan? Heaven knows. The swan is a luminous irrelevance, sailing for a moment into the picture with all its curves and its whiteness and its mythologies, and sailing out again to the strains of a defunctive music, fabulously mournful. Tennyson knew his magician's business.


> Now, as in Tullia's tomb, one lamp burned clear,
> Unchanged for fifteen hundred year,
> May these love-lamps we here enshrine
> In warmth, light, lasting, equal the divine.
>
> JOHN DONNE.

For purely magical reasons 'fifteen hundred' is one of the largest numbers in all our poetical arithmetic.

> Now, as in Tullia's tomb one lamp burned clear,
> Unchanged for fifteen hundred year . . .

The span of time is immense, appalling in its length. Paradoxically, 'fifteen thousand' would have been shorter. The very emphasis of that too loudly protesting *ou* detracts from the final effect. 'Thousand' puts us on our guard, sets up a reaction of scepticism; we

226

feel that the noisy diphthong is overdoing it.  Whereas
' hundred' is a muffled force, a power restrained and
silenced, but breaking through its gags.  ' Fifteen
hundred ' says more than the sound of its syllables wants
it to say ;  the sound of ' fifteen thousand ' wants to say
a great deal, but, protesting too much, says much less
than it intends.  Nor must we forget the effects of a
historical education.  ' Fifteen hundred ' is a real
historical period—a slice of time that begins with Minos
and ends with Augustus, or begins with Augustus and
ends with Lorenzo the Magnificent.  Whereas ' fifteen
thousand ' takes us clean out of bounds and lands us in
some dim cave or lake dwelling among heaven knows
what kind of gibbering savages.  Nevertheless, the fact
remains that it is the sound which matters more than
the history.  And the proof is that another poet has
used the same number no less effectively in a non-
historical context.  ' But when I see,' writes Mr.
W. H. Davies,

           the first time in my life,
Our Sussex downs, so mighty, strong and bare,
That many a wood of fifteen hundred trees
Seems but a handful scattered lightly there. . . .

The size of those woods is prodigious, and that of the
Sussex downs, in consequence, beyond all computation.
' Fifteen hundred ' is a magical number.


O si chère de loin et proche et blanche, si
Délicieusement toi, Mary, que je songe
A quelque baume rare émané par mensonge.
Sur aucun bouquetier de cristal obscurci.

227

Le sais-tu, oui ! pour moi voici des ans, voici
Toujours que ton sourire éblouissant prolonge
La même rose avec son bel été qui plonge
Dans autrefois et puis dans le futur aussi.

Mon cœur qui dans les nuits parfois cherche à s'entendre
Ou de quel dernier mot t'appeler le plus tendre
S'exalte en celui rien que chuchoté de sœur,

N'était, très grand trésor et tête si petite,
Que tu m'enseignes bien toute une autre douceur
Tout bas par le baiser seul dans tes cheveux dite.

STÉPHANE MALLARMÉ.

Mallarmé's sonnet is that miracle, an entire poem
consciously organized to such a pitch of artistic perfection that the whole is one single, unflawed piece of
' pure poetry.' In its unobtrusive way, this is one of
the most potent spells ever committed to paper. In
what does its magic consist ? Partly it is a magic of
sound. (Note, incidentally, that the magical sound is
not concentrated in single words, or phrases, or lines ;
it is the sound of the poem as a whole.) But mainly it is
a magic of grammar, a syntactical magic of the relations of thought with thought. Consider the sextet ;
it is a grammatical apocalypse. A whole world of
ideas is miraculously concentrated by means of the
syntax into what is almost a point. ' My heart, that in
the night-time sometimes seeks to understand itself or
by what last tenderest name to call you, exults in that
no more than whispered of sister, were it not, great
treasure and head so small, that you teach me quite
another sweetness, uttered softly in your hair by the

kiss alone.' The literal translation is absurd, but serves to bring to light the technique by means of which the grammatical magic is produced.

Another example of grammatical magic is furnished by Dante in that hell-conquering formula which Virgil addresses first to Charon, and then to Minos. The infernal rulers have raised objections to Dante's presence in hell. Virgil silences them thus :—

> Vuolsi così colà, dove si puote
> Ciò che si vuole ; e più non dimandare.

'Thus is it willed there, where what is willed can be done ; ask no more.'

The closely knit grammar-magic produces a sound-magic that reinforces its effect. Hearing the spell, Charon and Minos obey. We are not surprised.

> The maidens came
> When I was in my mother's bower ;
> I had all that I would.
> The bailey beareth the bell away ;
> The lily, the rose, the rose I lay.
>
> The silver is white, red is the gold ;
> The robes they lay in fold.
> The bailey beareth the bell away ;
> The lily, the rose, the rose I lay.
>
> And through the glass window shines the sun.
> How should I love, and I so young ?
> The bailey beareth the bell away ;
> The lily, the rose, the rose I lay.       ANON.

The magic here is the magic of obscurity. Who is

229

the bailey? Why does he bear away the bell? And does he do so in the old idiomatic sense of the phrase, or literally? And is ' the lily, the rose, the rose I lay ' merely a meaningless refrain, like ' butter and eggs and a pound of cheese ' ? Or does it express in flowery terms the fact that the speaker—presumably a very young bride awaiting her bridegroom—lies a virgin and blushing? These are questions which I shall probably never be in a position to answer. For the long poem, from which this often-quoted fragment is taken, has been printed in its entirety only in Volume cvii. of the *Archiv für das Studium der neueren Sprachen und Literaturen* ; and, frankly, I find it very difficult, almost impossible, to consult works of this kind. Which is, perhaps, all for the best. For if one really knew what this fragment was about, one might come to like it less. Uncomprehended, it is lovely, and mysteriously haunts the imagination with its peculiar magic. Let us leave well alone and be thankful for it.

> O blest unfabled Incense Tree,
> That burns in glorious Araby,
> With red scent chalicing the air,
> Till earth-life grow Elysian there !
>
> Half buried to her flaming breast
> In this bright tree, she makes her nest,
> Hundred-sunned Phoenix, when she must
> Crumble at length to hoary dust.
>
> Her gorgeous death-bed, her rich pyre
> Burnt up with aromatic fire !
> Her urn, sight high from spoiler men !
> Her birthplace, when self-born again !

The mountainless green wilds among,
Here ends she her unechoing song :
With amber tears and odorous sighs,
Mourned by the desert when she dies.

GEORGE DARLEY.

Every now and then, by some marvellous mistake, George Darley managed to concentrate his normal diffuseness ; and from out of the iridescent fog of his pleasant versifying would emerge, startlingly, a real poem. This is the best of them—a small masterpiece of condensed phrasing and rich precise imagery, magical with symbolism and obscure allusion. Darley seems to have used the Phoenix, as D. H. Lawrence used it, as a symbol of the physical desire that dies in flame and is born again in flame. That the scene of the Phoenix's death and birth should be a desert, green, indeed, but mountainless, and her song unechoing, is certainly significant—I suppose of the fact that physical desire, like virtue, is its own reward and end, that it leads to no eminences beyond the heights of passion and has no meaning outside itself.

Je suis le ténébreux, le veuf, l'inconsolé,
Le Prince d'Aquitaine à la tour abolie.
Ma seule étoile est morte, et mon luth constellé
Porte le soleil noir de la mélancolie.
Dans la nuit du tombeau toi qui m'as consolé,
Rend-moi le Pausilippe et la mer d'Italie,
La fleur qui plaisait tant à mon cœur désolé,
Et la treille où le pampre à la rose s'allie.
Suis-je Amour ou Phébus ? Lusignan ou Biron ?

231

Mon front est rouge encor du baiser de la reine.
J'ai rêvé dans la grotte où nage la Sirène,
Et j'ai deux fois vainqueur traversé l'Achéron,
Modulant tour à tour sur la lyre d'Orphée
Les soupirs de la sainte et les cris de la fée.

GÉRARD DE NERVAL.

De Nerval's is an incantation of the ' A-kid-I-fell-into-the-milk ' variety.  His magic, like Darley's, is the magic of symbols and allusions—only the symbols are more esoteric than Darley's straightforward Phoenix, the allusions are not to a philosophy but to events in the private life, perhaps even in the dream life, of the poet. Darley only suffered from a soul-disfiguring stammer. Nerval was eccentric to the point of occasional madness. He ended his life hanging from a lamp-post.  We divine in the obscure, private magic of the poem its author's suicidal loneliness and isolation.  The *Surréalistes*, and all those who without calling themselves by that name conform more or less completely to *surréaliste* practice, have methodized Nerval's madness. The impenetrable magic of private allusion and dream symbol—this is their classical style.

Gaze not on swans in whose soft breast
A full-hatched beauty seems to nest,
Nor snow which, falling from the sky,
Hovers in its virginity.

Gaze not on roses, though new-blown,
Graced with a fresh complexion,
Nor lilies which no subtle bee
Hath robbed by kissing-chemistry.

For if my emperess appears,
Swans moulting die, snow melts to tears,
Roses do blush and hang their heads,
Pale lilies shrink into their beds.

So have I seen stars big with light
Prove lanterns to the moon-eyed night.
Which, when Sol's rays were once displayed,
Sank in their sockets and decayed.

HENRY NOEL.

Mere lusciousness of sensuous imagery is magical.
Pleasurable sensations are supernatural in the sense that
they are beyond reason, cannot be analysed, or ex-
plained, or described—only experienced and then
named. The pleasures of looking at a swan and
stroking its feathers are as incommunicable as the
mystic vision. Poetry that effectively reminds us of
such pleasures partakes of their supernatural quality,
their magicalness. Thanks to the sumptuous shape of
swans and the softness of their plumes, and thanks to
the skill with which the poet has rendered this splendour
and deliciousness, the first stanza of Henry Noel's little
poem is genuinely magical. It tails off, as it proceeds,
into agreeable but unexciting ordinariness.

The drunkard now supinely snores,
His load of ale sweats through his pores ;
Yet when he wakes, the swine shall find
A crapula remains behind.
CHARLES COTTON.

Why is this quatrain so admirable ? Simply and
solely because of the crapula in line four. The word is

233

magical. Partly on account of its unfamiliarity. (The Americans who, since Prohibition, have developed so copious and expressive a vocabulary to describe the various phases of alcoholic intoxication, have overlooked ' crapula.' I recommend it to their attention.) Partly because it makes such an admirable noise. To be magical, unfamiliarity must be sonorous. The magic of ' crapula ' conjures up visions of a thoroughly disgusting lowness. It reminds us of creeping, of the American game with dice, of the verb to crap—derived from it, no doubt,—of the popular Press and the Papuan islanders, of crape and Crippen. A man with a crapula is manifestly and unquestionably a swine. The magicalness of single words varies in different countries. In English ears, for example, ' Rozanov ' has a most poetical sound. But Rozanov himself was constantly complaining of his misfortune in being burdened with so grotesque a name. And in Dostoevsky's *Possessed* there is evidently nothing specially ludicrous about the name of the old gentleman whom Stavrogin led by the nose. But for French and English readers Mr. Gaganov is the last word in absurdity. The rules of the literary Black Art are without universal validity ; each language has its own.

Lo ! Death has reared himself a throne
In a strange city lying alone
Far down within the dim West,
Where the good and the bad and the worst and the best
Have gone to their eternal rest.

There shrines and palaces and towers
(Time-eaten towers that tremble not !)
Resemble nothing that is ours.
Around, by lifting winds forgot,
Resignedly beneath the sky
The melancholy waters lie.
No rays from the holy heaven come down
On the long night-time of that town :
But light from out the lurid sea
Streams up the turrets silently—
Gleams up the pinnacles far and free—
Up domes, up spires, up kingly halls,
Up fanes, up Babylon-like walls,
Up shadowy long-forgotten bowers
Of sculptured ivy and stone flowers,
Up many and many a marvellous shrine
Whose wreathèd friezes intertwine
The viol, the violet and the vine.
Resignedly beneath the sky
The melancholy waters lie.
So blend the turrets and shadows there,
That all seem pendulous in air,
While from a proud tower in the town
Death looks gigantically down.
There open fanes and gaping graves
Yawn level with the luminous waves :
But not the riches there that lie
In each idol's diamond eye—
Not the gaily-jewelled dead
Tempt the waters from their bed :
For no ripples curl, alas !
Along that wilderness of glass—
No swellings tell that winds may be

Upon some far-off happier sea—
No heavings hint that winds have been
On seas less hideously serene.

But lo, a stir is in the air !
The wave—there is a movement there !
As if the towers had thrust aside,
In slightly sinking, the dull tide—
As if their tops had feebly given
A void within the filmy heaven.
The waves have now a redder glow,
The hours are breathing faint and low ;
And when, amid no earthly moans,
Down, down that town shall settle hence,
Hell, rising from a thousand thrones,
Shall do it reverence.

EDGAR ALLAN POE.

All the poems of Edgar Allan Poe are spells. A self-
conscious and scientific sorcerer, he was for ever experimentally combining in varying proportions the
different kinds of poetical magic—magic of sound,
magic of obscure allusion and private symbol, magic of
remoteness and fanciful extravagance. The results are
seldom entirely successful. He laid on the magic too
thick, and when spells are too abracadabrical, they do
not work. This ' City in the Sea ' is one of the few
really admirable poems which Poe ever wrote. It is
genuinely magical because its author has been so
sparing of his magics.

# MUSIC AND POETRY

The images, in terms of which poets have tried to render music—here is subject-matter for a most instructive thesis. It will not, alas, be written by me ; my own burrowings into literature have been too unsystematic to allow me to undertake such a labour. The most I can do is to hint at the way such a thesis might be written—to suggest provisionally, on the strength of my small knowledge of the subject, the sort of way in which a person who knew it thoroughly might organize his material. Music, then, has been rendered in poetry either by onomatopœic means, or else by means of images themselves non-musical. Of the onomatopœic means I need hardly speak. Very little can be done with mere noise. Browning's ' *Bangwhang-whang* goes the drum, *tootle-te-tootle* the fife,' does not, and is not meant to, give more than a perfunctorily comic rendering of the music of a band. Alliterative effects, like ' the moan of doves in immemorial elms, the murmur of innumerable bees,' are better, but do not go very far and will not stand frequent repetition. In order to express music in terms of their art, poets have had for the most part to rely on intrinsically non-musical images. These images, so far as my knowledge of the subject goes, always belong to one of three classes. The first, in terms of which poets express the quality of music and of the feelings which it rouses, is the class of purely sensuous images—most often of touch, but frequently also of sight, taste and smell. Here, to

illustrate my point, are three poetical renderings of
music by Strode, Herrick and Milton respectively.

> O lull me, lull me, charming air !
>   My senses rock with wonder sweet ;
> Like snow on wool thy fallings are ;
>   Soft like a spirit's are thy feet.
>     Grief who needs fear
>     That hath an ear ?
>       Down let him lie
>       And slumbering die,
> And change his soul for harmony.

WILLIAM STRODE.

> So smooth, so sweet, so silvery is thy voice,
> As, could they hear, the damned would make no
>     noise,
> But listen to thee (walking in thy chamber)
> Melting melodious words, to lutes of amber.

ROBERT HERRICK.

> Can any mortal mixture of earth's mould
> Breathe such divine enchanting ravishment ?
> Sure something holy lodges in that breast,
> And with these raptures moves the vocal air
> To testify his hidden residence.
> How sweetly did they float upon the wings
> Of silence, through the empty-vaulted night,
> At every fall smoothing the raven down
> Of darkness till it smiled ! I have oft heard
> My mother Circe with the Sirens three,
> Amidst the flowery-kirtled Naïades,
> Culling their potent herbs and baleful drugs,

238

Who, as they sung, would take the prisoned soul,
And lap it in Elysium : Scylla wept,
And chid her barking waves into attention,
And fell Charybdis murmured soft applause.
Yet they in pleasing slumber lulled the sense,
And in sweet madness robbed it of itself ;
But such a sacred and home-felt delight,
Such sober certainty of waking bliss,
I never heard till now.

JOHN MILTON.

Strode uses images of touch. Nothing could be *softer* than snow on wool unless it is a spirit's feet. Herrick mingles touch with taste and sight. The voice is smooth, sweet and silvery. The words melt—in the mouth, under the hand—and the sounds of the lute have the golden translucency of amber. Milton renders his music in terms of touch. Feathers replace the wool and snow of Strode—feathers, equally soft, but more glossy. The fingers slide, caressed and caressing ;

At every fall smoothing the raven down
Of darkness till it smiled.

How delicately voluptuous against the hand—against the cheek and lips—is that smooth dark touch of feathers ! And (miracle !) how near we are to music !

Crashaw's poem on the musical duel between a lutanist and a nightingale is a mine of such purely sensuous images.

She measures every measure, everywhere
Meets art with art ; sometimes as if in doubt,
Not perfect yet, and fearing to be out,
Trails her plain ditty in one long-spun note

239

Through the sleek passage of her open throat,
A clear unwrinkled song. . . .

Thread turns to silver wire : the fingers slide,
smoothly, smoothly, till the wire becomes a rod of
crystal, a fountain congealed—clear, unwrinkled—the
crystal melts to wetness ; we have 'slippery song,'
'lubric throat !' 'liquid melody,' Then, suddenly,
drought :

> In ripened airs
> A golden-headed harvest fairly rears
> His honey-dropping tops ;

The cool wet music has been modulated into warmth
and colour and sweetness and the sunshine of early
autumn. And so on, through sparklings and flashings
to a 'sea of Helicon,' to a sweetness 'softer than that
which pants in Hebe's cup.'

So much for purely sensuous images. The poet uses
them to render the quality of the immediate experience
of music. He finds them inadequate, however, when
he wants to express the significances and values of
music. To render these, he has recourse to two other
classes of images—images of Nature and images of
the Supernatural.

It is not only in 'some world far from ours' that

> . . . music and moonlight and feeling
> Are one.

They are also, as the practice of the poets shows,
mysteriously one even in this world. Consider these
lines from Shelley's 'The Woodman and the
Nightingale' :

240

A woodman, whose rough heart was out of tune,
(I think such hearts yet never came to good)
Hated to hear, under the stars or moon,

One nightingale in an interfluous wood
Satiate the hungry dark with melody ;—
And as a vale is watered by a flood,

Or as the moonlight fills the open sky
Struggling with darkness—as a tuberose
Peoples some Indian dell with scents which lie,

Like clouds above the flower from which they rose,
The singing of that happy nightingale
In this sweet forest, from the golden close

Of evening till the star of dawn may fail,
Was interfused upon the silentness.

It is evident that the poet feels the need to escape
from the implications of an almost suffocating nearness
and immediacy contained in the pure-sensuous images.
Music is more than a delicious stroking of feathers and
wool, more than a taste of honey, a gleam of amber and
silver. It leads the mind out of itself, gives it access to
a wider world,—to valleys (in Shelley's imagery) with
their lakes and streams, to open skies and moonlight.
Even the scent-image is associated with a landscape—
and a landscape, moreover, which imagination must
travel far to see ; for the dell which the tuberose
peoples with its odours is Indian.

Many of Shakespeare's numerous references to music
are associated in the poetical context with the grandeurs
and the serenities of Nature. I say 'associated with'
rather than ' rendered by,' because Shakespeare, so far

as my memory goes, never sets out to give a complete
poetic rendering of music. It was unnecessary ; he had
the real thing ready to hand—actors who could sing,
players of instruments. When he wanted to produce
the effects which belong to music alone, he produced
them directly, not at second hand, in the necessarily
inadequate terms of another art. Still, the circumstances in which he writes of music, the contexts in
which the word occurs, are significant. One remembers the last act of *The Merchant of Venice*.

> How sweet the moonlight sleeps upon this bank !
> Here will we sit, and let the sounds of music
> Creep in our ears ; soft stillness and the night
> Become the touches of sweet harmony.
> Sit, Jessica ; look, how the floor of heaven
> Is thick inlaid with patines of bright gold ;
> There's not the smallest orb which thou behold'st
> But in his motion like an angel sings,
> Still quiring to the young-eyed cherubins ;
> Such harmony is in immortal souls ;
> But, whilst this muddy vesture of decay
> Doth grossly close it in, we cannot hear it.

One remembers Oberon's speech to Puck in the
second act of *A Midsummer Night's Dream*.

> My gentle Puck, come hither. Thou remember'st
> Since once I sat upon a promontory,
> And heard a mermaid on a dolphin's back
> Uttering such dulcet and harmonious breath,
> That the rude sea grew civil at her song,
> And certain stars shot madly from their spheres
> To hear the sea-maid's music.

One remembers the dying Gaunt who speaks in one breath of ' the setting sun, and music at the close.' Night, the sea, stars and sunset—it is in terms of Nature at her serenest that Shakespeare expresses what music makes him feel. Nor is Shakespeare the only poet to go to Nature for expressive analogies to music.

' My spirit,' writes Shelley,

> My spirit like a charmèd bark doth swim
> Upon the liquid waves of thy sweet singing,
> Far far away into the regions dim
> Of Rapture—as a boat with swift sails winging
> Its way adown some many-winding river,
> Speeds through dark forests. . . .

The same image is developed at length in Asia's song from *Prometheus Unbound*.

> My soul is an enchanted boat,
> Which, like a sleeping swan, doth float
> Upon the silver waves of thy sweet singing :
> And thine doth like an angel sit
> Beside the helm conducting it,
> Whilst all the winds with melody are ringing.
> It seems to float ever, for ever,
> Upon that many-winding river,
> Between mountains, woods, abysses,
> A paradise of wildernesses !
> Till, like one in slumber bound,
> Borne to the ocean, I float down, around,
> Into a sea profound, of ever-spreading sound.

Readers of *A la Recherche du Temps Perdu* will remember the elaborate landscape-imagery in terms of which Proust tried to give a literary rendering of his

243

favourite music—tried, and was on the whole remarkably successful. Vinteuil's Sonata is almost, for a careful reader of Proust, a real piece of music. And here I take the opportunity of saying that this paper deals only with *successful* writers. It is, unnecessary, except perhaps in a systematic thesis, to quote from those who have tried to do the job and failed. To take a single example, Wordsworth is the author of a most elaborate ' Ode on the Power of Sound '—one of the worst poems ever written by a great man (and that, heaven knows, is saying a good deal). I might have quoted this piece—but only to demonstrate Wordsworth's complete and absolute failure to render in poetical terms either the quality of music, or its significance, or its value. Writing about negative quantities is uninteresting ;  I have confined myself to the more fruitful discussion of what actually exists.

It is time now to discuss the third class of images, in terms of which poets have expressed the quality and significance of music. Images of the Supernatural, as I have called them, abound in all poetical renderings of music. My first example is taken from *Prometheus Unbound*—from the song whose opening stanza appears on the preceding page. It will be seen that the images of Nature, with which the poem began, are gradually transformed into images of the Supernatural.

> Meanwhile thy spirit lifts its pinions
> In music's most serene dominions,
> Catching the winds that fan that happy heaven.
> And we sail on, away, afar,
> Without a course, without a star,

But by the instinct of sweet music driven ;
Till through Elysian garden islets,
By thee, most beautiful of pilots,
Where never mortal pinnace glided,
The boat of my desire is guided :
Realms where the air we breathe is love,
Which in the winds and on the waves doth move,
Harmonizing the earth with what we feel above.

We have passed Age's icy caves,
And Manhood's dark and tossing waves,
And Youth's smooth ocean, smiling to betray :
Beyond the glassy gulfs we flee
Of shadow-peopled Infancy,
Through Death and Birth to a diviner day :
A paradise of vaulted bowers
Lit by downward-gazing flowers,
And watery paths that wind between
Wildernesses calm and green,
Peopled by shapes too bright to see,
And rest, having beheld ;  somewhat like thee ;
Which walk upon the sea, and chant melodiously.

In another of Shelley's poems (' To Constantia,
Singing ') we find supernatural images following, not
on images of Nature, but on pure-sensuous images of
smell and touch.  The poet begins by expressing the
quality of the music heard, then passes to an interpretation, in the highest possible terms, of its significance.

Thus to be lost and thus to sink and die
Perchance were death indeed !—Constantia, turn !
In thy dark eyes a power like light doth lie,
Even though the sounds which were thy voice, which
   burn

Between thy lips, are laid to sleep ;
Within thy breath, and on thy hair, like odour, it is yet,
And from thy touch like fire doth leap.
Even while I write, my burning cheeks are wet ;
Alas, that the torn heart can bleed, but not forget !

A breathless awe, like the swift change
Unseen but felt in youthful slumbers,
Wild, sweet, but uncommunicably strange,
Thou breathest now in fast-ascending numbers.
The cope of heaven seems rent and cloven
By the enchantment of thy strain,
And on my shoulders wings are woven,
To follow its sublime career
Beyond the mighty moons that wane
Upon the verge of Nature's utmost sphere,
Till the world's shadowy walls are past and disappear.

Music, then, is another world—heavenly not only in
its profound, supernatural significance, but also in its
quality of immediate, sensuous delightfulness. (Lovers
also find their pleasures unearthly ; and in the
literature of religious mysticism intense sensations *are*
heaven). In rendering music, poets seem to turn quite
naturally to the Supernatural. It is almost casually and
in passing, as though the association of ideas were
perfectly obvious, that Chaucer brings together music
and heaven.

> Antigone the sheen
> Gan on a Trojan song to singen clear
> That it an heaven was her voice to hear.

Milton is more systematic and technical in his
employment of supernatural images.

There let the pealing organ blow
To the full-voicèd quire below,
In service high and anthems clear,
As may with sweetness, through mine ear,
Dissolve me into ecstasies,
And bring all heaven before mine eyes.

In ' At a Solemn Music ' he elaborates the theme and
presents us with an actual picture of that heaven which
the sweetness of music in the ear brings (such is the
magic of imagination) in moving forms and colours
before the eyes.

Blest pair of Sirens, pledges of Heaven's joy,
Sphere-born harmonious sisters, Voice and Verse,
Wed your divine sounds ; and mixed power employ
Dead things with inbreathed sense able to pierce,
And to our high-raised phantasy present
That undisturbèd song of pure concent
Aye sung before the sapphire-coloured throne
To Him that sits thereon,
With saintly shout and solemn jubilee ;
Where the bright seraphim in burning row
Their loud uplifted angel-trumpets blow,
And the cherubic host in thousand quires
Touch their immortal harps of golden wires,
With those just spirits that wear victorious palms,
Hymns devout and holy psalms
Singing everlastingly.

Crashaw speaks of ' ravished souls,' ' strong ecstasies '
that carry the spirit
                              through all the spheres
Of Music's heaven ; and seat it there on high
In th' empyrean of pure harmony.

For Dryden, harmony is ' heavenly harmony.'

> But O, what art can teach,
> What human voice can reach,
> The sacred organ's praise ?
> Notes inspiring holy love,
> Notes that wing their heavenly ways
> To mend the choirs above.
>
> Orpheus could lead the savage race ;
> And trees uprooted left their place,
> Sequacious of the lyre ;
> But bright Cecilia raised the wonder higher ;
> When to her organ vocal breath was given,
> An angel heard and straight appeared,
> Mistaking Earth for Heaven.

Cowley, in the first book of his ' Davideis,' has a digression on music which I like extremely for its ingenious absurdity and which I quote, because the absurdity has something genuinely poetical about it and because the whole passage illustrates yet once more the tendency of poets to speak of music in terms of the Supernatural.

> Tell me, O Muse (for thou, or none, canst tell
> The mystic powers that in blest numbers dwell,
> Thou their great nature knowest, nor is it fit
> This noblest gem of thine own crown to omit),
> Tell me from whence these heavenly charms arise ;
> Teach the dull world to admire what they despise.
> As first a various unformed hint we find
> Rise in some god-like poet's fertile mind,
> Till all the parts and words their places take,
> And with just marches verse and music make :--

248

Such was God's poem, this world's new essay ;
So wild and rude in its first draft it lay.
The ungoverned parts no correspondence knew,
An artless war from thwarting motions grew ;
Till they to number and fixt rules were brought
By the eternal Mind's poetic thought.
Water and Air he for the tenor chose,
Earth made the base, the treble Flame arose ;
To the active Moon a quick brisk stroke he gave,
To Saturn's string a touch more soft and grave.
The motions straight and round, and swift, and slow,
And short, and long, were mixt and woven so,
Did in such artful figures smoothly fall,
As made this decent measured dance of All.
And this is Music : sounds that charm our ears
Are but one dressing that rich science wears.
Though no man hear't, though no man it rehearse,
Yet will there still be music in my verse.
In this Great World so much of it we see,
The Lesser, man, is all o'er harmony.
Storehouse of all proportions ! single quire !
Which first God's breath did tunefully inspire !
From hence blest Music's heavenly charms arise,
From sympathy which them and man allies.
Thus they our souls, thus they our bodies win,
Not by their force, but party that's within.
Thus when two brethren strings are set alike,
To move them both, but one of them we strike.


One could multiply examples ; but I have quoted
enough, I think, to make my original point clear :
when pure-sensuous images prove inadequate, poets

249

have recourse to images of Nature and images of the Supernatural.

Certain poets, more knowledgeable than the majority of their kind in the theory and practice of the sister art, have tried, from time to time, to give a direct and technical rendering of music. A passage in the eleventh book of *Paradise Lost* is famed among musicians for its concentrated accuracy.

> His volant touch,
> Instinct through all proportions low and high,
> Fled and pursued transverse the resonant fugue.

' Fled and pursued '—the words describe to a nicety the entries and developments of the various themes. ' Transverse ' expresses the fact that the music is polyphonic rather than homophonic; horizontal, not vertical. And ' resonant ' taken in its strict, etymological meaning, implies the repetitions which are the essence of fugal form. To a reader who knows what a fugue is, the lines conjure up very precisely a certain kind of music. Browning did something similar in his ' Master Hugues of Saxe-Gotha.' More elaborately and diffusely, and on the whole less successfully, he tried to render in terms half musical-technical, half dramatic, the essence of an imaginary fugue—a fugue, moreover, as he implies, intrinsically rather dull in its elaborate polyphony. The poem has most of the defects of Browning—from literariness, and excessive facility, to an entire lack of the ' magical ' quality and of that penetrative force, that ' X-radiance,' which only a concentrated aptness of stylistic beauty can give—

most of the defects, I repeat, and very few of Browning's
compensating merits. I shall leave it unquoted. A
much more successful attempt in the same kind is his
' Toccata of Galuppi.'

What? Those lesser thirds so plaintive, sixths,
    diminished, sigh on sigh,
Told them something? Those suspensions, those
    solutions—' Must we die? '
Those commiserating sevenths—' Life might last!
    we can but try.'

' Were you happy? '—' Yes.'—' And are you still as
    happy? '—' Yes. And you? '
—' Then more kisses! '—' Did *I* stop them, when a
    million seemed so few? '
Hark, the dominant's persistence till it must be
    answered to!

So, an octave struck the answer. Oh, they praised
    you, I dare say!
' Brave Galuppi! that was music! good alike at
    grave and gay!
I can always leave off talking when I hear a master
    play! '

Then they left you for their pleasure : till in due
    time, one by one,
Some with lives that came to nothing, some with
    deeds as well undone,
Death stepped tacitly and took them where they
    never see the sun.

But when I sit down to reason, think to take my stand
    nor swerve,

While I triumph o'er a secret wrung from Nature's
    close reserve,
In you come with your cold music, till I creep thro'
    every nerve.

Yes, you, like a ghostly cricket, creaking where a
    house was burned :
' Dust and ashes, dead and done with, Venice spent
    what Venice earned,
The soul, doubtless, is immortal—where a soul can
    be discerned.'

ROBERT BROWNING.

Of all the poets Browning and Milton seem to have
been the two who understood music the best.   In that
lovely passage from ' Comus,' which is quoted on an
earlier page, Milton says something which proves him
a real and complete musician—one who loved music
with all his mind as well as with his heart and the
lower viscera (the organs most in request among
listeners).   ' Yet they,' he writes, referring to Circe and
the three Sirens,

> Yet they in pleasing slumber lulled the sense,
> And in sweet madness robbed it of itself ;
> But such a sacred and home-felt delight,
> Such sober certainty of waking bliss,
> I never heard till now.

' Such sober certainty of waking bliss '—it is the
perfect statement of what one feels when one is listening to the slow movement of the Ninth Symphony, to
the Mass in D, to Mozart's Requiem or *Ave Verum Corpus*
to any work into which a great man and a consummate

musician (and, alas, how few of them there are !) has put the whole of his being.

Some people love music, not wisely, but too well. Even among the musically talented and well-educated you will find them. I know several, excellent performers and widely read, whose passion for music is such, that it robs them of their judgment. The sensuous pleasures which they derive from harmonious sounds as such, the emotional excitements into which almost any of the devices of composition can throw them—these are so intense that they can listen happily to works which, judged by the highest standards, are obviously not of the highest quality.

For them, music which

> in pleasing slumber lulls the sense,
> And in sweet madness robs it of itself,

is just as satisfactory as the music that appeals to all the highest faculties of the spirit and so keeps the listener in a tense and focussed state of 'waking bliss.' One can love music gluttonously and voluptuously (and I have known people whose appetite for sweet sounds was positively hoggish), or one can love it with heart, soul and mind, as a complete and fully developed human being. Milton, it is evident, loved in this latter way.

> Nor cold, nor stern, my soul ! yet I detest
> These scented rooms where, to a gaudy throng,
> Heaves the proud harlot her distended breast
> In intricacies of laborious song.

253

These feel not Music's genuine power, nor deign
  To melt at Nature's passion-warbled plaint ;
But when the long-breathed singer's uptrilled strain
  Bursts in a squall, they gape for wonderment.
                            SAMUEL TAYLOR COLERIDGE.

The concentrated femaleness of most contralto voices
is, I admit, a most distressing thing.  Coleridge has
perfectly expressed those emotions of dismay, embarrass-
ment and indignation, which we have all so often felt
while listening to a murderous rendering of even
Schubert or Wolff.

But how deeply I distrust the judgment of people who
talk about ' Nature's passion-warbled plaint ' and dis-
parage the intricacies of musical art !  They are the
sort of people whose bowels yearn at the disgusting
caterwaulings of Tziganes ;  who love to listen to
Negroes and Cossacks ;  who swoon at the noises of the
Hawaiian guitar, the Russian balalaika, the Argentine
saw and even the Wurlitzer organ ;  who prefer the
simpleminded sadness, the rustically trampling merri-
ment of English folk-songs to *Figaro* or the Mass in D.
In other words, they are the sort of people who don't
really like music.

# THE REST IS SILENCE

Think not it was those colours, red and white,
Laid but on flesh that could affect me so,
But something else, which thought holds under lock
And hath no key of words to open it.
They are the smallest pieces of the mind
That pass the narrow organ of the voice ;
The great remain behind in that vast orb
Of the apprehension, and are never born.

MICHAEL DRAYTON.

If all the pens that ever poets held
Had fed the feeling of their masters' thoughts,
And every sweetness that inspired their hearts,
Their minds and muses, on admired themes ;
If every heavenly quintessence they still
From their immortal flowers of poesy,
Wherein, as in a mirror, we perceive
The highest reaches of a human wit ;
If these had made one poem's period,
And all combined in beauty's worthiness,
Yet should there hover in their restless heads
One thought, one grace, one wonder at the least
Which into words no virtue can digest.

CHRISTOPHER MARLOWE.

I swear I will never henceforth have to do with the
     faith that tells the best !
I will have to do only with that faith that leaves the
     best untold.          WALT WHITMAN.

Whitman here succumbs to his besetting sin and
protests too much.  For why this swearing, unless for

255

mere emphatic swearing's sake ? Oath or no oath, the best, as also the worst, *cannot* be told—can only be experienced. Dante did not find it necessary to swear not to tell the best about Paradise. 'O ben creato spirito,' he wrote :—

> O ben creato spirito, che ai rai
>   di vita eterna la dolcezza senti,
>   che non gustata non s'intende mai. . . .

He knew that there were certain ' sweets which, untasted, may never be understood.' So did Marlowe and Drayton. And so, indeed, must all who have ever wrestled with the problem of artistic expression.

However miraculously endowed a poet may be, there is always, beyond the furthest reach of his powers of expression, a great region of the unexpressed and inexpressible. The rest is always silence.

# GOD

The thoughts which the word, God, suggests to the human mind are susceptible of as many varieties as human minds themselves.  The Stoic, the Platonist and the Epicurean, the Polytheist, the Dualist and the Trinitarian, differ infinitely in their conceptions of its meaning.  They agree only in considering it the most awful and most venerable of names, as a common term to express all of mystery, or majesty, or power which the invisible world contains.  And not only has every sect distinct conceptions of the application of this name, but scarcely two individuals of the same sect, who exercise in any degree the freedom of their judgment, or yield themselves with any candour of feeling to the influencings of the visible world, find perfect coincidence of opinion to exist between them.

PERCY BYSSHE SHELLEY.

The worship of God is : Honouring His gifts in other men, each according to his genius, and loving the greatest men best ; those who envy or calumniate great men hate God, for there is no other God.

The Angel, hearing this, almost became blue ; but mastering himself he grew yellow and at last white, pink and smiling.

WILLIAM BLAKE.

I know of no other Christianity and no other Gospel than the liberty both of body and mind to exercise the Divine Arts of Imagination. . . . The Apostles knew of no other Gospel.  What were all

257

their spiritual gifts ? What is the Divine Spirit ? Is the Holy Ghost any other than an Intellectual Fountain ? What is the Harvest of the Gospel and its Labours ? What is that Talent which it is a curse to hide ? What are the treasures of Heaven which we are to lay up for ourselves, are they any other than Mental Studies and Performances ? What are all the Gifts of the Gospel, are they not all Mental Gifts ? What is the Joy of Heaven but improvement in the things of the Spirit ? What are the Pains of Hell but Ignorance, Bodily Lust, Idleness and devastation of the things of the spirit ?

Answer this to yourselves, and expel from among you those who pretend to despise the Labours of Art and Science, which alone are the Labours of the Gospel. Is not this plain and manifest to the thought ? Can you think at all and not pronounce heartily : That to labour in Knowledge is to build up Jerusalem, and to Despise Knowledge is to Despise Jerusalem and her builders.

**WILLIAM BLAKE.**

# DISTRACTIONS

O knit me that am crumbled dust ! the heap
  Is all dispersed and cheap.
Give for a handful but a thought,
   And it is bought.
    Hadst thou
Made me a star, a pearl or a rainbow,
  The beams I then had shot
  My light had lessened not ;
    But now
I find myself the less the more I grow.
   The world
Is full of voices ; man is called and hurled
  By each ; he answers all,
  Knows every note and call ;
    Hence still
Fresh dotage tempts or old usurps his will.
Yet hadst thou clipt my wings when coffined in
   This quickened mass of sin,
And saved that light, which freely thou
  Didst then bestow,
   I fear,
I should have spurned and said thou didst forbear
  Or that thy store was less ;
  But now since thou didst bless
   So much,
I grieve, my God, that thou hast made me such.
   I grieve ?
O, yes ! thou know'st I do ; come, and relieve
And tame and keep down with thy light
Dust that would rise and dim the sight,

Lest left alone too long
Amidst the noise and throng,
  Oppressed I,
Striving to save the whole, by parcels die.
HENRY VAUGHAN.

Leave, leave thy gadding thoughts ;
    Who pores
    And spies
  Still out of door,
    Descries
  Within them nought.

The skin and shell of things,
    Though fair,
    Are not
  Thy wish nor prayer,
    But got
  By mere despair
    Of wings.

To rack old elements
    Or dust
    And say :
  Sure here he must
    Needs stay,
  Is not the way,
    Nor just.
HENRY VAUGHAN.

Fate which foresaw
How frivolous a baby man would be—
By what distractions he would be possessed,
How he would pour himself in every strife,
And well nigh change his own identity—
That it might keep from his capricious play

His genuine self, and force him to obey
Even in his own despite his being's law,
Bade through the deep recesses of our breast
The unregarded river of our life
Pursue with indiscernible flow its way ;
And that we should not see
The buried stream, and seem to be
Eddying at large in blind uncertainty,
Though driving on with it eternally.

But often, in the world's most crowded streets,
But often in the din of strife,
There rises an unspeakable desire
After the knowledge of our buried life ;
A thirst to spend our fire and restless force
In tracking out our true, original course ;
A longing to enquire
Into the mystery of this heart which beats
So wild, so deep in us—to know
Whence our lives come, and where they go.
And many a man in his own breast then delves
But deep enough, alas ! none ever mines.
And we have been on many thousand lines,
And we have shown, on each, spirit and power ;
But hardly have we, for one little hour,
Been on our own line, have we been ourselves—
Hardly had skill to utter one of all
The nameless feelings that course through our
     breast ;
But they course on for ever unexpressed.
And long we try in vain to speak and act
Our hidden self, and what we say and do
Is eloquent, is well—but 'tis not true !
And then we will no more be racked

With inward striving, and demand
Of all the thousand nothings of the hour
Their stupefying power ;
Ah yes, and they benumb us at our call !
Yet still, from time to time, vague and forlorn,
From the soul's subterranean depth upborne
As from an infinitely distant land,
Come airs, and floating echoes, and convey
A melancholy into all our day.
Only—but this is rare—
When a belovèd hand is laid in ours,
When, jaded with the rush and glare
Of the interminable hours,
Our eyes can in another's eyes read clear,
When our world-deafened ear
Is by the tones of a loved voice caressed—
A bolt is shot back somewhere in our breast.
And a lost pulse of feeling stirs again.
The eye sinks inward, and the heart lies plain,
And what we mean, we say, and what we would,
    we know.
A man becomes aware of his life's flow,
And hears its winding murmur ;  and he sees
The meadows where it glides, the sun, the breeze.

And there arrives a lull in the hot race
Wherein he doth for ever chase
That flying and elusive shadow, rest.
An air of coolness plays upon his face,
And an unwonted calm pervades his breast.
And then he thinks he knows
The hills where his life rose,
And the sea where it goes.

MATTHEW ARNOLD.

Cette source de mort, cette homicide peste,
Ce péché, dont l'enfer a le monde infecté,
M'a laissé pour tout être un bruit d'avoir été,
Et je suis de moi-même une image funeste.
L'Auteur de l'Univers, le Monarque céleste,
S'était rendu visible en ma seule beauté ;
Ce vieux titre d'honneur qu'autrefois j'ai porté
Et que je porte encore est tout ce qui me reste.
Mais c'est fait de ma gloire et je ne suis plus rien
Qu'un fantôme qui court après l'ombre d'un bien
Ou qu'un corps animé du seul ver qui le ronge.
Non, je ne suis plus rien, quand je veux m'éprouver,
Qu'un esprit ténébreux qui voit tout comme en songe,
Et cherche incessamment ce qu'il ne peut trouver.

JEAN OGIER DE GOMBAULD.

The subject of distractions is one that has greatly pre-occupied every moralist with a contemplative turn of mind. Of all the treatments of the theme with which I am acquainted, the best, the most reasonable and scientific is to be found in the *Journal Intime* of Maine de Biran (October 9th, 1817). He begins by quoting Pascal :—

' Man is more to be pitied for being able to distract himself with things so frivolous and low than for grieving over his real miseries ; and his amusements are infinitely less reasonable than his melancholy (*ennui*).'

' But reason,' is Maine de Biran's comment, ' has nothing to do either with *ennui* or the propensity to amusements. These are purely organic dispositions, to which will and reason can oppose ideas, but which

263

they can neither change nor directly combat. When I am organically sad and bored, no amusements, no ideas can change this fundamental state of my being—though it is possible for me to be, to a certain extent, distracted. When my organism is in good condition, everything becomes an amusement and a pleasure—everything from external sensations and *far niente* to ideas. Pascal is surely quite wrong in all that he says about the cause of human wretchedness and of that perpetual agitation in which men pass their lives. Preoccupied solely with his design, which is to show that humanity has fallen and that it was created for a better state, Pascal treats a man as a simple subject and takes no account whatever of the influence of his organic states on his immediately experienced feeling of existence. This feeling may be happy or unhappy, sad or pleasant ; and he experiences it in spite of all amusements, he experiences it as much when he does not want to think of himself as when he is reduced to doing so. . . .

' " The soul," says Pascal in another place, " finds nothing in herself to be pleased with—sees nothing but what, when she thinks of it, distresses her. This is what forces the soul to launch herself abroad. Busying herself with outward things, she seeks to forget her true condition. Her joy consists in this forgetfulness. To make her wretched, it is enough to compel her to look at herself and have no company but her own. . . . Men bustle about and load themselves with business, they think incessantly of their money and their honour, or of those of their friends ; what a strange way, you will say, of trying to make oneself happy ! What more could one do to make oneself miserable ? Do you ask what one could do ? One could deliver men from all these cares ; for then they would see themselves, they would think of what they are ; and that, precisely, is what they cannot bear. That is why, after all their business, if they have a little leisure, they try to waste that too in some amusement that will allow them to escape from themselves. . . . Men's dislike of repose arises from the weakness of our condition and from another effective cause, which is this : our weak and mortal condition is so wretched that, when nothing prevents us from thinking of it, and we see nothing but ourselves, nothing can console us."

'One would say (after reading this) that the removal of all causes of external sensation or amusement was enough to turn every individual into a deep thinker busy with self-analysis, with meditations on life and death and all that is most distressing in the condition of humanity. But to meditate thus one must put forth more effort, more intellectual activity than is necessary to follow the course of all the affairs of ordinary life. The activity which makes us think of ourselves is only a mode of that activity which, according to Pascal, prevents us from thinking of ourselves. If every mental labour tends only to steal us from ourselves, then we can only think of ourselves in order to forget our own existence, to distract ourselves from ourselves. The contradiction is strange and inexplicable.

'Banish all sensuous impressions, every cause of

movement ; for such men as know and love only the life of sensation, life will become a hideous blank, a complete negation of existence. But for those who are accustomed to intellectual life, thought will fill this void, or render it imperceptible. Even when they meditate on the nothingness of man, they will be leading a full life. The others will be unhappy, not because they have to think of themselves or their wretched condition, but because they can think of nothing at all. Capable only of feeling, they are unhappy when the customary stimulants of sensibility are removed. Pascal would have understood this well enough, if he had not been preoccupied with the idea of the fall of man, and the notion that man experiences an intimate feeling of his degradation whenever he is not distracted from without. But we find nothing of the kind in ourselves. It is only the philosophers who conceive, by dint of meditation, a better or higher state.'

Quand chez les débauchés l'aube blanche et vermeille
Entre en société de l'idéal rongeur,
Par l'opération d'un mystère vengeur,
Dans la brute assoupie un Ange se réveille.

CHARLES BAUDELAIRE.

Quand le ciel bas et lourd pèse comme un couvercle
Sur l'esprit gémissant en proie aux longs ennuis,
Et que de l'horizon embrassant tout le cercle
Il nous verse un jour noir plus triste que les nuits ;

Quand la terre est changée en un cachot humide,
Où l'espérance, comme une chauve-souris,

S'en va battant les murs de son aile timide
Et se cognant la tête à des plafonds pourris ;

Quand la pluie étalant ses immenses traînées
D'une vaste prison imite les barreaux,
Et qu'un peuple muet d'infâmes araignées
Vient tendre ses filets au fond de nos cerveaux ;

Des cloches tout à coup sautent avec furie
Et lancent vers le ciel un affreux hurlement,
Ainsi que des esprits errants et sans patrie
Qui se mettent à geindre opiniâtrément.

Et de longs corbillards, sans tambours ni musique,
Défilent lentement dans mon âme ; l'Espoir,
Vaincu, pleure, et l'Angoisse atroce, despotique,
Sur mon crâne incliné plante son drapeau noir.

CHARLES BAUDELAIRE.

As well in his life as in his lyrics, Baudelaire illustrates the generalizations formulated by Maine de Biran. The organic state of debauchees at dawn is such, that angels cannot help waking up in them. What were, a few hours before, temptations have utterly ceased to tempt. Nothing, not the most expensive of champagnes, not the loveliest and most willing of ladies, could possibly distract them, at six in the morning, from their serious reflections on their own sorry condition and the *misère de l'homme*. And what bustle of business or of pleasure could bring any alleviation to the lot of one who suffers what in my second extract the poet so magnificently describes himself as suffering ?

It was in physiological terms—as the spleen or the black bile—that our fathers spoke of these states of misery. They may have been wrong in their choice of the offending organ ; but they were quite right in their insistence that some organ or other was generally responsible. Such morbid conditions as *accidie* are seldom on the same plane as the spiritual remedies prescribed by the moralists.

Lord, with what care hast Thou begirt us round !
Parents first season us ; then schoolmasters
Deliver us to laws ; they send us bound
To rules of reason, holy messengers ;
Pulpits and Sundays, sorrow dogging sin,
Afflictions sorted, anguish of all sizes,
Fine nets and stratagems to catch us in,
Bibles laid open, millions of surprises,
Blessings beforehand, ties of gratefulness,
The sound of glory ringing in our ears ;
Without, our shame ; within, our consciences ;
Angels and grace, eternal hopes and fears.
  Yet all these fences and their whole array
  One cunning bosom-sin blows quite away.

GEORGE HERBERT.

# AMOR FATI

Weighing the steadfastness and state
Of some mean things which here below reside,
Where birds, like watchful clocks, the noiseless date
    And intercourse of times divide,
Where bees at night get home and hive, and flowers,
    Early as well as late,
Rise with the sun, and set in the same bowers ;

I would, said I, my God would give
The staidness of these things to man ! for these
To his divine appointments always cleave,
    And no new business breaks their peace :
The birds nor sow nor reap, yet sup and dine ;
    The flowers without clothes live,
Yet Solomon was never dressed so fine.

Man hath still either toys or care :
But hath no root, nor to one place is tied,
But ever restless and irregular,
    About this earth doth run and ride.
He knows he hath a home, but scarce knows where ;
    He says it is so far,
That he has quite forgot how to go there.

He knocks at all doors, strays and roams ;
Nay, hath not so much wit as some stones have,
Which, in the darkest nights, point to their homes,
    By some hid sense their Maker gave.
Man is the shuttle, to whose winding quest
    And passage through these looms
God ordered motion, but ordained no rest.

HENRY VAUGHAN.

It is man's intelligence that makes him so often behave more stupidly than the beasts. An animal is without even the semblance of free will. Predestined by its instincts, it has no choice. In every circumstance it must do the thing that the age-long experience of its species has found to be, on the whole, most profitable for specific survival. Judged by utilitarian standards, what it does is, generally, the right thing. (This applies, of course, only to the animal's behaviour in, statistically speaking, 'normal' circumstances. In circumstances that are to any considerable extent unlike average circumstances, the animal almost always does the hopelessly wrong thing.)

Man is so intelligent that he feels impelled to invent theories to account for what happens in the world. Unfortunately, he is not quite intelligent enough, in most cases, to find correct explanations. So that when he acts on his theories, he behaves very often like a lunatic. Thus, no animal is clever enough, when there is a drought, to imagine that the rain is being withheld by evil spirits, or as a punishment for its transgressions. Therefore you never see animals going through the absurd and often horrible fooleries of magic and re-ligion. No horse, for example, would kill one of its foals in order to make the wind change its direction. Dogs do not ritually urinate in the hope of persuading heaven to do the same and send down rain. Asses do not bray a liturgy to cloudless skies. Nor do cats attempt, by abstinence from cat's meat, to wheedle the feline spirits into benevolence. Only man behaves with such gratuitous folly. It is the price he has to pay for being intelligent, but not, as yet, quite intelligent enough.

> Heaven, what an age is this ! what race
>   Of giants are sprung up that dare
> Thus fly in the Almighty's face
>   And with his Providence make war.
>
> I can go nowhere but I meet
>   With malcontents and mutineers,
> As if in life was nothing sweet,
>   And we must blessings reap in tears.
>
> O senseless Man that murmurs still
>   For happiness, and does not know,
> Even though he might enjoy his will,
>   What he would have to make him so !
>
> CHARLES COTTON.

The workmanship of souls is by the inaudible words
    of the earth ;
The great masters know the earth's words and use
    them more than the audible words. . . .

The Earth does not argue,
Is not pathetic, has no arrangements,
Does not scream, haste, persuade, threaten, promise,
Makes no discriminations, has no conceivable failures,
Closes nothing, refuses nothing, shuts none out
Of all the powers, objects, states, it notifies, shuts none
    out.

The Earth does not exhibit itself, nor refuse to exhibit
    itself—possesses still underneath ;
Underneath the ostensible sounds, the august chorus
    of heroes, the wail of slaves,

Persuasions of lovers, curses, gasps of the dying,
 laughter of young people, accents of bargainers,
Underneath these, possessing the words that never
 fail.

To her children, the words of the eloquent dumb
 great Mother never fail,
The true words do not fail, for motion does not fail,
 and reflection does not fail ;
Also day and night do not fail, and the voyage we
 pursue does not fail.

WALT WHITMAN.

How fevered is the man who cannot look
Upon his mortal days with temperate blood,
Who vexes all the leaves of his life's book,
And robs his fair name of its maidenhood ;
It is as if the rose should pluck herself,
Or the ripe plum finger its misty bloom,
As if a Naiad, like a meddling elf,
Should darken her pure grot with muddy gloom ;
But the rose leaves herself upon the briar,
For winds to kiss and grateful bees to feed,
And the ripe plum still wears its dim attire,
The undisturbèd lake has crystal space ;
Why then should man, teasing the world for
 grace,
Spoil his salvation for a fierce miscreed ?

JOHN KEATS.

That great poets should be capable of making such
enormous errors of judgment as most of them in fact do
make—some with an appalling frequency—is, for me,

a subject of chronic astonishment. How was it possible, for example, that a man of Keats's literary sensibility could find it in him to spoil an otherwise admirable sonnet with that hideously inappropriate and ugly seventh line?

As if a Naiad, like a meddling elf, . . .

Isn't it manifestly obvious that Naiads and elves, in the particular poetical circumstances, are completely out of place? The whole point of the sonnet lies in its opposition of Man, discontented and self-tortured, to a Nature that is calm and that accepts its fate (for the good reason, incidentally, that it is mindless and cannot do otherwise). Himself a meddling elf, Keats has ruined the whole idea by introducing into the world of Nature a piece of ridiculous supernatural machinery. What he meant to say was : ' As if the clear lake should stir up its own mud.' What the exigences of rhyme and a fatal itch to be too ' poetical ' actually made him say was :—

As if a Naiad, like a meddling elf,
Should darken her pure grot with muddy gloom.

It is a wound and an affront. One winces, one could groan, and one wants to break out into abusive curses.

As proude Bayard ginneth for to skippe
Out of the wey, so priketh him his corn,
Till he a lash have of the longe whippe,
Than thenketh he, ' though I praunce al biforn
First in the trace, ful fat and newe shorn,

273

Yet I am but an hors and horses law
I moot endure and with my feres draw.'

So fared it by this fierce and proude knight.
GEOFFREY CHAUCER.

It would be wearisome if the greater were invariably illustrated by the less, the higher always by the lower. But, occasionally, how stimulatingly astringent is a cockney metaphor! Even James Joyce's 'snot-green sea' has something to be said for it.

It is characteristic of Chaucer that he should liken the hero of his romance to a corn-fed horse that has to be whipped into good behaviour. Sermons in dogs, books in the quacking ducks. . . . The father of English poetry was a naturalist.

# STRENUOUS LIFE

Give me a spirit that on this life's rough sea,
Loves to have his sails filled with a lusty wind,
Even till his sail-yards tremble, his masts crack,
And his rapt ship run on her side so low
That she drinks water and her keel ploughs air.
There is no danger to a man that knows
What life and death is ; there's not any law
Exceeds his knowledge ; neither is it lawful
That he should stoop to any other law.

GEORGE CHAPMAN.

Comme je descendais des Fleuves impassibles,
Je ne me sentis plus guidé par les haleurs :
Des peaux-rouges criards les avaient pris pour cibles
Les ayant cloués nus aux poteaux de couleurs.

J'étais insoucieux de tous les équipages,
Porteur de blés flamands ou de cotons anglais.
Quand avec mes haleurs ont fini ces tapages,
Les Fleuves m'ont laissé descendre ou je voulais. . .

Plus douce qu'aux enfants la chair des pommes sures,
L'eau verte pénétra ma coque de sapin
Et des taches de vins bleus et des vomissures
Me lava, dispersant gouvernail et grappin.

Et dès lors je me suis baigné dans le poème
De la mer infusé d'astres et lactescent,
Dévorant les azurs verts où, flottaison blême
Et ravie, un noyé pensif parfois descend. . . .

Je sais les cieux crevant en éclairs, et les trombes,
Et les ressacs, et les courants ; je sais le soir,

L'aube exaltée ainsi qu'un peuple de colombes,
Et j'ai vu quelquefois ce que l'homme a cru voir.

J'ai vu le soleil bas taché d'horreurs mystiques,
Illuminant de longs figements violets,
Pareils à des acteurs de drames très antiques,
Les flots roulant au loin leurs frissons de volets. . . .

J'ai heurté, savez-vous ? d'incroyables Florides
Mêlant aux fleurs des yeux de panthères, aux peaux
D'hommes, des arcs-en-ciel tendus comme des brides,
Sous l'horizon des mers, à des glauques troupeaux.

J'ai vu fermenter les marais, énormes nasses
Où pourrit dans les joncs tout un Léviathan :
Des écroulements d'eau au milieu de bonaces,
Et les lointains vers les gouffres cataractant ;

Glaciers, soleils d'argent, flots nacreux, cieux de
      braises,
Echouages hideux au fond des golfes bruns,
Où les serpents géants dévorés de punaises
Choient des arbres tordus avec de noirs parfums. . . .

Or moi, bateau perdu sous les cheveux des anses,
Jeté par l'ouragan dans l'éther sans oiseau,
Moi dont les Monitors et les voiliers des Hanses
N'auraient pas repêché la carcasse ivre d'eau,

Moi qui tremblais, sentant geindre à cinquante lieues
Le rut des Béhémots et des Maelstroms épais,
Fileur éternel des immobilités bleues,
Je regrette l'Europe aux anciens parapets.

J'ai vu des archipels sidéraux, et des îles
Dont les cieux délirants sont ouverts au vogueur :
Est-ce en ces nuits sans fond que tu dors et t'exiles,
Million d'oiseaux d'or, ô future Vigueur ?

Mais, vrai, j'ai trop pleuré.   Les aubes sont navrantes,
Toute lune est atroce et tout soleil amer.
L'âcre amour m'a gonflé de torpeurs enivrantes.
Oh, que ma quille éclate ! Oh, que j'aille à la mer !

Si je désire une eau d'Europe, c'est la flache
Noire et froide où, vers le crépuscule embaumé,
Un enfant accroupi, plein de tristesse, lâche
Un bateau frêle comme un papillon de mai.

Je ne puis plus, baigné de vos langueurs, ô lames,
Enlever leur sillage aux porteurs de cotons,
Ni traverser l'orgueil des drapeaux et des flammes,
Ni nager sous les yeux horribles des pontons.

ARTHUR RIMBAUD.

### The Pulley

When God at first made man,
Having a glass of blessings standing by,
Let us, said He, pour on him all we can ;
Let the world's riches which dispersèd lie
    Contract into a span.

So strength first made a way,
Then beauty flowed, then wisdom, honour, pleasure :
When almost all was out, God made a stay,
Perceiving that alone of all his treasure,
    Rest in the bottom lay.

For if I should, said He,
Bestow this jewel also on my creature,
He would adore my gift instead of me,
And rest in Nature, not the God of Nature ;
    So both should losers be.

277

Yet let him keep the rest,
But keep them with repining restlessness ;
Let him be rich and weary, that at least,
If goodness lead him not, yet weariness
    May toss him to my breast.
                                        GEORGE HERBERT.


Lord, what a busy restless thing
    Hast thou made man !
Each day and hour he is on the wing,
    Rests not a span.
Hadst thou given to this active dust
    A state untired,
The lost son had not left the husk,
    Nor home desired.
That was thy secret, and it is
    Thy mercy too ;
For when all fails to bring to bliss,
    Then this must do.
O Lord, and what a purchase will that be,
To take us sick, that, sound, would not take thee !
                                        HENRY VAUGHAN.


So many people are ill and overworked, that Paradise
is commonly conceived as a place of repose.  But there
are hours and days, there are even whole epochs in the
life of every human being, when George Herbert's
Pulley simply doesn't pull ; when rest is the last thing
of which the soul and body feel a need ; when all desire
tends quiveringly towards a strenuous and exciting
heaven.

    ' Art thou weary, art thou languid, art thou sore
distrest ? '  The answer to the hymn-writer's question

is : Yes, sometimes ; but sometimes not at all. Christianity has always found a certain difficulty in fitting the unfatigued, healthy and energetic person into its philosophical scheme. Whenever they come across such a person, its moralists begin by reminding him that, even if he does happen to be feeling well now, he will very soon be old and decrepit. After which they tell him that he ought, whatever the state of his mind and his viscera, to behave as though he were feeling ill. ' Sickness,' said Pascal, who was never afraid of carrying arguments to their logical conclusions, ' sickness is the Christian's natural state ; for in sickness a man is as he ought always to be—in a state, that is to say, of suffering, of pain, of privation from all the pleasures of the senses, exempt from all passions.' The good Christian who has the misfortune to be hale should turn himself into an artificial invalid. But as Kierkegaard remarks, ' to be healed by the help of Christianity is not the difficulty ; the difficulty is to become thoroughly sick.' For all people at some times, and for some people at all times, this difficulty is insuperable. ' Million d'oiseaux d'or, ô future Vigueur ! ' Even here and now, vigour can be like the sudden explosion above a rock in the sea—the sudden explosion, the continued swoop and glitter—of innumerable wings.

> Over hills and uplands high
> Hurry me, Nymphs ! O hurry me !
> Where green Earth from azure sky
> Seems but one blue step to be :

Where the sun his wheel of gold
Burnishes deeply in her mould,
And her shining walks uneven
Seem declivities of heaven.
Come, where high Olympus nods,
Ground-sill to the hall of Gods !
Let us through the breathless air
Soar insuperable, where
Audibly in mystic ring
The angel orbs are heard to sing ;
And from that bright vantage ground
Viewing nether heaven profound,
Mark the eagle near the sun
Scorching to gold his pinions dun ;
With fleecy birds of paradise
Up floating to their native skies :
Or hear the wild swans far below
Faintly whistle as they row
Their course on the transparent tide
That fills the hollow welkin wide.


Light-skirt dancers, blithe and boon,
With high hosen and low shoon,
'Twixt sandal bordure and kirtle rim
Showing one pure wave of limb,
And frequent to the cestus fine
Lavish beauty's undulous line,
Till like roses veiled in snow
'Neath the gauze your blushes glow ;
Nymphs, with tresses which the wind
Sleekly tosses to his mind,
More deliriously dishevelled
Than when the Naxian widow revelled

With her flush bridegroom on the ooze,
Hurry me, Sisters ! where ye choose.

GEORGE DARLEY.

Paradise may be the imagination of what we have
not, or else the apotheosis of what we have.  Rimbaud's
million of golden birds were his own vigour of body and
mind, his own passionate life, refined and indefinitely
intensified.  In *Bateau Ivre* he affirmed himself.

Hopelessly imprisoned within his stammer, timid, a
sedentary, Darley created his paradise by a process, not
of affirmation, but of negation.  All that was not his
actual physique, character and way of living was
heaven.  The two poets set out in diametrically
opposite directions ;  their destination, however, was
the same.

# MISERY

*The Teacher's Monologue*

The room is quiet, thoughts alone
   People its mute tranquillity ;
The yoke put off, the long task done,—
   I am, as it is bliss to be,
Still and untroubled.  Now I see,
   For the first time, how soft the day
O'er waveless water, stirless tree,
   Silent and sunny, wings its way.
Now as I watch that distant hill,
   So faint, so blue, so far removed,
Sweet dreams of home my heart may fill,
   That home, where I am known and loved. . . .
Sometimes I think a narrow heart
   Makes me thus mourn those far away,
And keeps my love so far apart
   From friends and friendships of to-day ;
Sometimes I think 'tis but a dream
   I treasure up so jealously ;
All the sweet thoughts I live on seem
   To vanish into vacancy ;
And then this strange coarse world around
   Seems all that's palpable and true,
And every sight and every sound
   Combine my spirit to subdue
To aching grief ;  so void and lone
   Is Life, and Earth—so worse than vain
The hopes that, in my own heart sown
   And cherished by such sun and rain
As Joy and transient Sorrow shed,

Have ripened to a harvest there :
Alas ! methinks I hear it said,
   ' Thy golden sheaves are empty air.'
CHARLOTTE BRONTË.


Though but a shadow, but a sliding,
  Let me know some little joy ;
  We that suffer long annoy
  Are contented with a thought,
  Through an idle fancy wrought :
O let my joys have some abiding !
FRANCIS BEAUMONT.


To toil, to think, to long, to grieve—
  Is such my future fate ?
The morn was dreary ; must the eve
  Be also desolate ?
Well, such a life at least makes Death
  A welcome, wished-for friend ;
Then, aid me, Reason, Patience, Faith,
  To suffer to the end !
CHARLOTTE BRONTË.


No worst, there is none.  Pitched past pitch of grief,
More pangs will, schooled at forepangs, wilder wring.
Comforter, where, where is your comforting ?
Mary, mother of us, where is your relief ?
My cries heave, herds-long ; huddle in a main, a
    chief
Woe, world-sorrow ; on an age-old anvil wince and
    sing—
Then lull, then leave off.  Fury had shrieked, 'No ling-
ering !  Let me be fell : force I must be brief !'

O the mind, mind has mountains ; cliffs of fall
Frightful, sheer, no-man-fathomed. Hold them
    cheap
May who ne'er hung there. Nor does long our small
Durance deal with that steep or deep. Here ! creep,
Wretch, under a comfort serves in a whirlwind : all
Life death does end and each day dies with sleep.

                GERARD MANLEY HOPKINS.

Alliteration ; successions of consonant-clotted mono-
syllables ; Lydgate-like breakings and prolongings of
the line—it is by such devices that Hopkins contrives
to render (with what terrible adequacy) the sobbing and
spasmodic extremes of unhappiness.

Charlotte Brontë was but an indifferent poet. The
two extracts quoted above happen to be admirable ;
but that is more by luck than good management. All
her verse has a deadness and a flatness about it. It so
happens that the subject matter of the pieces I have
quoted demands a dead, flat treatment. Charlotte
Brontë gives it this treatment, for the good reason that
she can give it no other. In a work of art, success is
always admirable, whatever the means by which it is
achieved. The long-drawn dreariness of a day-to-day
existence felt to be uncongenial and degrading has
seldom been better rendered than in ' The Teacher's
Monologue.'

In some ways, I think, this dull chronic misery is
worse than the paroxysms of unhappiness expressed by
Hopkins. Griefs ' pitched past pitch of grief ' are, by the
very extremity of their sharpness, quickening ; the
daily dreariness mutes and muffles the life within us till

284

we feel ourselves hideously diminished, less than human. There are worse pangs than this sense of sub-humanity ; but, just because they are worse, preferable. Yes, preferable ; for a moment at least, until our 'small durance' is exhausted and we fall, for a moment we shall be as superhuman as the ordeal through which we have to pass. It is by his superhuman moments that man lives.

# ESCAPE

The wind sounds only in opposing straits,
The sea, beside the shore ; man's spirit rends
Its quiet only up against the ends
Of wants and oppositions, loves and hates,
Where, worked and worn by passionate debates,
And losing by the loss it apprehends,
The flesh rocks round, and every breath it sends
Is ravelled to a sigh.  All tortured states
Suppose a straitened place.  Jehovah Lord,
Make room for rest around me ! out of sight
Now float me, of the vexing land abhorred,
Till in deep calms of space my soul may right
Her nature, shoot large sail on lengthening cord,
And rush exultant on the infinite.

ELIZABETH BARRETT BROWNING.

For thousand-fold are the troubles that the body
gives us . . . It fills us full of loves and lusts and fears,
with all kinds of delusions and rank nonsense ; and
in very truth, as men say, it so disposes us, that we
cannot think wisely at all. . . . We must set the soul
free of it ; we must behold things as they are, and then,
belike, we shall attain the wisdom that we desire and of
which we say we are lovers ; not while we live, but
after death, as the argument shows. . . . For then,
and not till then, will the soul be parted from the
body and exist in herself alone.

PLATO.

I love all waste
And solitary places, where we taste
The pleasure of believing what we see

Is boundless, as we wish our souls to be :
And such was this wide ocean, and this shore
More barren than its billows.

PERCY BYSSHE SHELLEY.

We spun

A shroud of talk to hide us from the sun
Of this familiar life, which seems to be
But is not—or is but quaint mockery
Of all we would believe, and sadly blame
The jarring and inexplicable frame
Of this wrong world :—and then anatomize
The purposes and thoughts of men whose eyes
Were closed in distant years ;—or widely guess
The issue of the earth's great business,
When we shall be as we no longer are—
Like babbling gossips safe, who hear the war
Of winds, and sigh, but tremble not.

PERCY BYSSHE SHELLEY.

La chair est triste, hélas ! et j'ai lu tous les livres.
Fuir ! là-bas fuir ! je sens que des oiseaux sont ivres
D'être parmi l'écume inconnue et les cieux !
Rien, ni les vieux jardins reflétés par les yeux
Ne retiendra ce cœur qui dans la mer se trempe,
O nuits ! ni la clarté déserte de ma lampe
Sur le vide papier que la blancheur défend,
Et ni la jeune femme allaitant son enfant.
Je partirai ! Steamer, balançant ta mâture,
Lève l'ancre pour une exotique nature !
Un Ennui, désolé par de cruels espoirs,
Croit encore à l'adieu suprême des mouchoirs !
Et, peut-être, les mâts, invitant les orages
Sont-ils de ceux qu'un vent penche sur les naufrages

Perdus, sans mâts, sans mâts, ni fertiles îlots. . . .
Mais, ô mon cœur, entends le chant des matelots !
STÉPHANE MALLARMÉ.

*Fuir, là-bas fuir*—it is what all of us aspire to do at
certain moments, what some of us are trying to do all
the time. The world in which our bodies are condemned to live is really too squalid, too vulgar, too
malignant to be borne. There is no remedy save in
flight. But whither ?

There are various possible retreats. The safest of
them, as Plato insists, is death.

> Fear no more the heat o' the sun,
> Nor the furious winter's rages.

For most people, however, death seems to be too
finally sovereign a remedy for the evils of living. They
know that, sooner or later, it will duly be administered ;
but they are not prepared to make the ultimate escape
before escape is forced upon them. What they want is a
death-surrogate in their lives—a state of being that
combines the advantages of being alive with those of
having removed to another world.

There are escapes into drink, into sensuality, into
play, into day-dreaming. None of these, however,
provides the perfect refuge. Lust exhausts itself ;
there are nights of self-questioning insomnia after
the day-dreams, mornings of sick repentance after the
alcohol ; as for play, only an imbecile could bear to
play away his existence. No ; of all the death-
surrogates incomparably the best is what is called—
rightly, after all—the higher life. Religious meditation,

288

scientific experiment, the acquisition of knowledge, metaphysical thinking and artistic creation—all these activities enhance the subjective sense of life, but at the same time deliver their practitioners from the sordid preoccupations of common living. They live, abundantly ; and they are, in the language of religion, ' dead to the world.' What could be more satisfactory ?

> ' Do you not hear the Aziola cry ?
>   Methinks she must be nigh,'
>     Said Mary, as we sate
> In dusk, ere stars were lit or candles brought :
>     And I, who thought
> This Aziola was some tedious woman.
>   Asked, ' Who is Aziola ? ' How elate
> I felt to know that it was nothing human,
>   No mockery of myself to fear or hate !
>     And Mary saw my soul,
> And laughed, and said, ' Disquiet yourself not ;
>   'Tis nothing but a little downy owl.'
>                               PERCY BYSSHE SHELLEY.

The flight in this case is to the world of animals. It is one of the most popular refuges. ' I think,' says Walt Whitman,

> I think I could turn and live with animals, they are
>   so placid and self-contained.
> I stand and look at them sometimes half the day long.
> They do not sweat and whine about their condition,
> They do not lie awake in the dark and weep for their
>   sins,

They do not make me sick discussing their duty to
    God.
Not one is dissatisfied, not one is demented with the
    mania of owning things,
Not one kneels to another, nor to his kind that lived
    thousands of years ago,
Not one is respectable and industrious over the whole
    earth.
So they show their relations to me, and I accept them,
They bring me tokens of myself, they evince them
    plainly in their possession.

Much more cogent than any that Whitman has
adduced, there is another reason why people take
refuge among the beasts. Many more men and women
leave the world for the kennel than for the cloister, and
with good cause ; in the kennel, even the feeblest and
dullest of human beings can feel himself the master, the
genius, positively the god. What a delightful, what an
intoxicating change from a world where unsympa-
thetic men exploit the weak and deride the stupid !

Disappointed humans discover among the fleas and
the dog-dung a kind of paradise of wish-fulfilment.
They are grateful to their pets—hysterically so at times,
almost insanely.

I call to mind in what state my soul once was, when
I dwelt in my monastery ; how then it was superior to
all transitory matters and how it would soar above
things corruptible.

                            GREGORY THE GREAT.

Behold him, priests, and though he stink of sweat,
Disdain him not ; for shall I tell you what ?
Such climb to heaven before the shaven crowns.
But how ? Forsooth, with true humility.
Not that they hoard their grain when it is cheap,
Not that they kill the calf to have the milk,
Not that they set debate between their lords
By earing up the balks that part their bounds ;
Not for because they can both crouch and creep
(The guilefull'st men that ever God yet made)
When as they mean most mischief and deceit ;
Not that they can cry out on landlords loud,
And say they rack their rents an ace too high,
When they themselves do sell the landlord's lamb
For greater price than ewe was wont be worth ;
But for they feed with fruits of their great pains
Both king and knight and priests in cloister pent.
Therefore I say that sooner some of them
Shall scale the walls that lead us up to heaven
Than corn-fed beasts, whose belly is their God,
Although they preach of more perfection.

GEORGE GASCOIGNE.

There can be no higher living that is not based solidly
upon an income. Gregory's soul was able to soar,
because the monastery provided his body with food
and clothing, and because numerous peasants and
artisans toiled in the welter of things corruptible in
order to provide the monastery with the means to
provide Gregory. These are facts which, however deep
our devotion to the things of the spirit, we must never
forget. Spirituality can so easily be made an excuse for
the most shocking sins, both of omission and commission.

Realistic humanism has no more dangerous enemy
than that speculative idealism, or 'spiritualism,'
which in place of the real individual man sets up the
consciousness or mind.

KARL MARX.

' None can usurp this height,' returned that shade,
' But those to whom the miseries of the world
Are misery, and will not let them rest.
All else who find a haven in the world,
Where they may thoughtless sleep away their days,
If by a chance into this fane they come,
Rot on the pavement, where thou rotted'st half.'
' Are there not thousands in the world,' said I,
Encouraged by the sooth voice of the shade,
' Who love their fellows even unto the death,
Who feel the giant agony of the world,
And more, like slaves to poor humanity,
Labour to mortal good ?  I sure should see
Other men here, but I am here alone.'
' Those whom thou spak'st of are no visionaries,'
Rejoined that voice, ' they are no dreamers weak,
They seek no wonder but the human face,
No music but a happy-noted voice—
They come not here, for thou art less than they.
What benefit canst thou do, or all thy tribe,
To the great world ?  Thou art a dreaming thing,
A fever of thyself ;  think of the earth ;
What bliss, even in hope, is there for thee ?
What haven ?  every creature hath its home,
Every sole man hath days of joy and pain,
Whether his labours be sublime or low—
The pain alone, the joy alone, distinct :

Only the dreamer venoms all his days,
Bearing more woe than all his sins deserve.
Therefore, that happiness be somewhat shared,
Such things as thou art are admitted oft
Into like gardens thou didst pass erewhile,
And suffered in these temples : for that cause
Thou standest safe beneath the statue's knees.'

JOHN KEATS.

These things, Ulysses,
The wise Bards also
Behold and sing.
But oh, what labour !
O Prince, what pain !

They too can see
Tiresias :—but the Gods
Who gave them vision,
Added this law :
That they should bear too
His groping blindness,
His dark foreboding,
His scorned white hairs ;
Bear Hera's anger
Through a life lengthened
To seven ages.

They see the Centaurs
On Pelion :—then they feel,
They too, the maddening wine
Swell their large veins to bursting : in wild pain
They feel the biting spears
Of the grim Lapithæ and Theseus drive,
Drive crashing through their bones ; they feel
High on a jutting rock in the red stream

Alcmena's dreadful son
Ply his bow :—such a price
The Gods exact for song ;
To become what we sing.

MATTHEW ARNOLD.

Artists are higher livers—dead, while they labour, to the world. Sometimes, however, some of them begin to question their right to be so happily defunct ; they wonder if it isn't somehow rather immoral to exist apart, as they do, in the heaven of the mind. It was a sense that they had no right to be posthumous spirits during their life-time, it was a twinge, so to say, of their physiological consciences, that drove Blake and D. H. Lawrence to preach a personal salvation through the body as well as the soul—a salvation that is, fundamentally and essentially, sexual salvation.

Faced by the same moral problem, Keats and Matthew Arnold developed a social conscience.

And can I ever bid these joys farewell ?
Yes, I must pass them for a nobler life,
Where I may find the agonies, the strife
Of human hearts.

They felt that it was their duty somehow to take their share in the sufferings and struggles of ordinary men and women living in the ordinary world of affairs. Arnold went so far in the direction of lower living as to become an inspector of schools. Keats, who had started his career in the medley and had hastily retired, felt it incumbent upon him to participate at least theoretically in its discomforts and its horrors. Both poets

tried to set their consciences at rest by insisting that the
artist who realizes imaginatively the pains of all the
world suffers more than the common man who bears
(but in the flesh) only his own particular pain. The
poet's greater capacity for suffering becomes, for such
potential ascetics, his moral justification, the reason for
his existence.

Some poets have participated less platonically in the
activities of the lower life. Milton, for example, began
above the medley ; conscious of his powers, deliberately planning his poetical career, he cultivated his
leisure in a next world of intellectual detachment.
What seemed a higher duty beckoned from the world of
the lower life. Milton went down unhesitatingly into
the arena, and there, in the battle, unhesitatingly
sacrificed his eyes.

> What supports me, dost thou ask ?
> The conscience, friend, to have lost them, overplied
> In Liberty's defence, my noble task,
> Of which all Europe rings from side to side.

Blind and in his old age, Milton returned again to the
other world of thought and imagination. Rimbaud,
on the contrary, never returned. 'Je ne pouvais pas
continuer,' he said to his sister, ' Je serais devenu fou et
puis . . . c'était mal.' It is not right for a poet to
penetrate so far into the other world as Rimbaud did.
Rather Aden and Abyssinia than such a dangerous, such
an immoral paradise. Rather death itself, with all the
pain and bitterness of dying, than this too delicious
death-surrogate.

# SERENITY

As when it happeneth that some lovely town
Unto a barbarous besieger falls,
Who there by sword and flame himself installs
And, cruel, it in tears and blood doth drown ;
Her beauty spoiled, her citizens made thralls,
His spite yet so cannot her all throw down,
But that some statue, arch, fane of renown
Yet lurks unmaimed within her weeping walls :
So, after all the spoil, disgrace and wrack,
That time, the world and death could bring
    combined,
Amidst that mass of ruins they did make,
Safe and all scarless yet remains my mind.
    From this so high transcending rapture springs
    That I, all else defaced, not envy kings.
                WILLIAM DRUMMOND.

Nîmes, Arles, Orange, Verona, Rome itself—where
had Drummond seen one of those great ruins of grey or
russet stone, towering up, symbolic, from out of the
noisy squalor of the modern town ?

‘ Safe and all scarless yet remains my mind.’ The
image of the aqueduct, the amphitheatre, the still un-
subverted triumphal arch is beautifully apt. It is a
pity that Drummond did not know how to do more
with this lovely invention. His sonnet is only respectable. I quote it for the sake of what it might have
been.

The poem of Matthew Arnold which follows is built
round a similar and equally beautiful image.

296

# SERENITY

Set where the upper streams of Simois flow
Was the Palladium, high 'mid rock and wood ;
And Hector was in Ilium there below,
And fought, and saw it not, but there it stood.

It stood ; and sun and moonshine rained their light
On the pure columns of its glen-built hall.
Backward and forward rolled the waves of fight
Round Troy ; but while this stood, Troy could not
    fall.

So, in its lovely moonlight, lives the soul.
Mountains surround it, and sweet virgin air ;
Cold plashing, past it crystal waters roll ;
We visit it by moments, ah ! too rare.

Men will renew the battle in the plain
To-morrow ; red with blood will Xanthus be ;
Hector and Ajax will be there again ;
Helen will come upon the wall to see.

Then we shall rust in shade, or shine in strife,
And fluctuate 'tween blind hopes and blind despairs,
And fancy that we put forth all our life,
And never know how with the soul it fares.

Still doth the soul, from its lone fastness high,
Upon our life a ruling effluence send ;
And when it fails, fight as we will, we die ;
And while it lasts, we cannot wholly end.

MATTHEW ARNOLD.

297

# DEATH

Come, lovely and soothing Death,
Undulate round the world, serenely arriving,
    arriving,
In the day, in the night, to all, to each,
Sooner or later, delicate Death.

Praised be the fathomless universe
For life and joy, and for objects and knowledge
    curious ;
And for love, sweet love—But praise ! O praise and
    praise
For the sure-enwinding arms of cool-enfolding Death.

Dark Mother, always gliding near, with soft feet,
Have none chanted for thee a chant of fullest
    welcome ?
Then I chant it for thee—I glorify thee above all ;
I bring thee a song, that, when thou must indeed
    come, thou come unfalteringly.

Approach, encompassing Death—strong deliveress !
When it is so—when thou hast taken them, I joyously
    sing the dead
Lost in the loving, floating ocean of thee,
Laved in the flood of thy bliss, O Death.

                              WALT WHITMAN.

Death is before me to-day,
Like the recovery of a sick man,
Like going forth into a garden after sickness ;
Death is before me to-day,
Like the odour of myrrh,
Like sitting under the sail on a windy day ;

Death is before me to-day,
Like the odour of lotus flowers,
Like sitting on the shore of drunkenness ;
Death is before me to-day,
Like the course of the freshet,
Like the return of a man from the war-galley to his
house,
When he has spent years in captivity.

EGYPTIAN POEM.

Accustom thyself to the thought that death is
nothing in relation to us ; for good and evil consist
in our perception of them, and death is the depriva-
tion of all perception. Hence the right understanding of this truth that death is nothing to us makes us
capable of enjoying this mortal life, not in setting
before ourselves the prospect of an endless time, but
in taking away from us the longing for immortality.
For there is nothing terrible in life for him who has
truly grasped that there is nothing in the beyond life.
Therefore he is foolish who says that death should be
feared, not because it will be painful when it comes,
but because it is painful to look forward to ; for it is
vain to be grieved in anticipation of that which
distresses us not when present. Thus, that which is
the most awful of evils, death, is nothing to us, since
when we exist there is no death, and when there is
death we no more exist. Death, then, is neither for
the living nor the dead, since it does not exist for the
former and the latter are no more.

EPICURUS.

Oh, for the time when I shall sleep
Without identity,
And never care how rain may steep,

Or snow may cover me !
No promised heaven these wild desires
Could all, or half, fulfil ;
No threatened hell, with quenchless fires,
Subdue this quenchless will !

So say I, and still say the same ;
Still, to my death, will say—
Three gods within this little frame
Are warring night and day ;
Heaven could not hold them all, and yet
They all are held in me,
And must be mine, till I forget
My present entity !
Oh, for the time, when in my breast
Their struggles will be o'er !
Oh, for the day, when I shall rest,
And never suffer more !

EMILY BRONTË.

Since Nature's works be good, and death doth serve
As Nature's work, why should we fear to die ?
Since fear is vain, but when it may preserve,
Why should we fear that which we cannot fly ?
Fear is more pain than is the pain it fears,
Disarming human minds of native might ;
While each conceit an ugly figure bears,
Which were not evil, well viewed in reason's light.
Our owly eyes, which dimmed with passions be,
And scarce discern the dawn of coming day,
Let them be cleared, and now begin to see
Our life is but a step in dusty way.
    Then let us hold the bliss of peaceful mind ;
    Since this we feel, great loss we cannot find.

SIR PHILIP SIDNEY.

Non è viltà, ne da viltà procede
S'alcun, per evitar più crudel sorte,
Odia la propria vita e cerca morte,
Se senza alcun rimedio il suo mal vede.
Ma bene è vil chi senza affanno crede
Travagliar manco in vita, e si conforte
Dicendo : io vivo. Ah menti poco accorte,
Che hanno in fedel morte poco fede !

Meglio è morire all'animo gentile
Che sopportar inevitabil danno
Che lo farria cambiar animo e stile.
Quanti ha la morte già tratti d'affanno !
Ma molti ch'hanno il chiamar morte a vile,
Quanto talor sia dolce ancor non sanno.

GIULIANO DE' MEDICI.

*Stile*—it is for that word that I like the sonnet. For the man of the Renaissance, even suicide is a matter of style. Living is a process of creation. Every life is a work of art and every spirit has its own distinguishing style, good or, more often, alas, indifferent or downright bad. Some people exist Miltonically and some Wilcoxically ; some in the style of *Figaro*, others in that of *The Merry Widow*. The noble soul is born and bred to live the equivalent of a Piero della Francesca fresco or a statue by Donatello. But, like every other art, the art of life can be practised well only when external circumstances are tolerably propitious. If circumstances change so much for the worse that the grand manner must be abandoned, then—for this particular noble spirit, at any rate—there is no alternative but suicide. Rather death than a style debased and made vulgar.

# CONCLUSIONS

Was it a dream ?  We sailed, I thought we sailed,
Martin and I, down a green Alpine stream,
Bordered, each bank, with pines ;  the morning sun,
On the wet umbrage of their glossy tops,
On the red pinings of their forest floor,
Drew a warm scent abroad ;  behind the pines
The mountain skirts, with all their sylvan change
Of bright-leafed chestnuts and mossed walnut trees
And the frail scarlet-berried ash, began.
Swiss chalets glittered on the dewy slopes,
And from some swarded shelf, high up, there came
Notes of wild pastoral music—over all
Ranged, diamond-bright, the eternal wall of snow.
Upon the mossy rocks at the stream's edge,
Backed by the pines, a plank-built cottage stood,
Bright in the sun ;  the climbing gourd-plant's leaves
Muffled its walls, and on the stone-strewn roof
Lay the warm golden gourds ;  golden, within,
Under the eaves, peered rows of Indian corn.
We shot beneath the cottage with the stream.
On the brown, rude-carved balcony, two forms
Came forth—Olivia's, Marguerite ! and thine.
Clad were they both in white, flowers in their breast ;
Straw hats bedecked their heads, with ribbons blue,
Which danced and on their shoulders, fluttering,
        played.
They saw us, they conferred ;  their bosoms heaved,
And more than mortal impulse filled their eyes.
Their lips moved ;  their white arms, waved eagerly,
Flashed once, like falling streams ;  we rose, we gazed.
One moment on the rapid's top our boat

Hung poised—and then the darting river of Life
(Such now, methought, it was) the river of Life,
Loud thundering bore us by ; swift, swift it foamed,
Black under cliffs it raced, round headlands shone.
Soon the planked cottage by the sun-warmed pines
Faded—the moss—the rocks ; us burning plains,
Bristled with cities, us the sea received.

MATTHEW ARNOLD.

Pour l'enfant amoureux de cartes et d'estampes,
L'univers est égal à son vaste appétit.
Ah, que le monde est grand à la clarté des lampes !
Aux yeux du souvenir que le monde est petit !

CHARLES BAUDELAIRE.

Enough, we live !—and if a life,
With large results so little rife,
Though bearable, seem hardly worth
This pomp of worlds, this pain of birth ;
Yet, Fausta, the mute turf we tread,
The solemn hills around us spread,
This stream which falls incessantly,
The strange-scrawled rocks, the lonely sky,
If I might lend their life a voice,
Seem to bear rather than rejoice.
And even could the intemperate prayer
Man iterates, while these forbear,
For movement, for an ampler sphere,
Pierce Fate's impenetrable ear ;
Not milder is the general lot
Because our spirits have forgot,
In action's dizzying eddy whirled,
The something that infects the world.

MATTHEW ARNOLD.

303

Here, in this little Bay,
Full of tumultuous life and great repose,
Where, twice a day,
The purposeless glad ocean comes and goes,
Under high cliffs and far from the huge town,
I sit me down.
For want of me the world's course will not fail ;
When all its work is done, the lie shall rot ;
The truth is great and shall prevail,
When none cares whether it prevail or not.

COVENTRY PATMORE.

### Timber

Sure thou didst flourish once ! and many springs,
Many bright mornings, much dew, many showers
Passed o'er thy head : many light hearts and wings,
Which now are dead, lodged in thy living bowers.
And still a new succession sings and flies ;
Fresh groves grow up and their green branches shoot
Towards the old and still enduring skies,
While the low violet thrives at their root.

HENRY VAUGHAN.

The thought that the world persists and, like the
Jolly Miller of the song, cares for nobody, is sometimes
profoundly consoling, sometimes a kind of derisive
insult. It depends upon circumstances and our mood.
Anyhow, the fact remains.

If dead we cease to be, if total gloom
    Swallow up life's brief flash for aye, we fare
As summer gusts, of sudden birth and doom,
    Whose sound and motion not alone declare,

But are their whole of being.　If the breath
　Be life itself, and not its task and tent,
If even a soul like Milton's can know death ;
　O man, thou vessel purposeless, unmeant,
Yet drone-hive strange of phantom purposes !
　Surplus of nature's dread activity,
Which, as she gazed on some nigh-finished vase
Retreating slow, with meditative pause,
　She formed with restless hands unconsciously !
Blank accident ! nothing's anomaly !
　If rootless thus, thus substanceless thy state,
Go, weigh thy dreams, and be thy hopes, thy fears,
The counter weights ! Thy laughter and thy tears
　Mean but themselves, each fittest to create
And to repay the other.　Why rejoices
　Thy heart with hollow joy for hollow good ?
Why cowl thy face beneath the mourner's hood,
Why waste thy sighs and thy lamenting voices,
Image of image, ghost of ghostly elf,
That such a thing as thou feel'st warm or cold ?
Yet what and whence thy gain, if thou withhold
　These costless shadows of thy shadowy self ?
Be sad ! be glad ! be neither ! seek, or shun !
Thou hast no reason why ! Thou canst have none,
Thy being's being is contradiction.
                    SAMUEL TAYLOR COLERIDGE.


I have never found any great difficulty in believing
that ' our laughter and our tears mean but themselves.' Nor, having formulated it, do I find the belief
particularly depressing.

No doubt it is because I am not depressed that I
believe.　Most of philosophy begins with a feeling or an

idiosyncrasy of temperament, and ends in a concept. Thus, men desire immortality and, having desired, set out to prove that they desire something real. The fact that they desire it is even used as an argument in favour of the existence of the object of desire. It is, indeed, *the* argument of the philosophers of immortality. Not, alas, a very cogent argument, except for those who already accept the conclusion, to which it is supposed to lead.

Reason, an Ignis Fatuus in the mind,
Which, leaving light of nature, sense, behind,
Pathless and dangerous wandering ways it takes
Through error's fenny bogs and thorny brakes,
Whilst the misguided follower climbs in vain
Mountains of whimsies heaped in his own brain ;
Stumbling from thought to thought, falls headlong
    down
Into doubt's boundless sea, where, like to drown,
Books bear him up a while and make him try
To swim with bladders of philosophy,
In hopes still to o'ertake the skipping light.
The vapour dances in his dazzling sight,
Till, spent, it leaves him to eternal night.
Then old age and experience, hand in hand,
Lead him to death, and make him understand,
After a search so painful and so long,
That all his life he had been in the wrong ;
Huddled in dirt, the reasoning engine lies,
Who was so proud, so witty and so wise.

JOHN WILMOT, EARL OF ROCHESTER.

The sun and stars that float in the open air ;
The apple-shaped earth and we upon it—surely the
    drift of them is something grand !
I do not know what it is, except that it is grand, and
    that it is happiness,
And that the enclosing purport of us here is not a
    speculation, or bon mot, or reconnaissance,
And that it is not something which by luck may turn
    out well for us, and without luck must be a
    failure for us,
And not something which may yet be retracted in a
    certain contingency.

                  WALT WHITMAN.

Reason emerges scatheless from Rochester's attack, which is directed in reality only against man's habit of reasoning on inadequate data. Reason is an instrument, which like any other instrument can be used well or ill. (The better the instrument, the more damage it can do when badly handled. A sharp saw will cut fingers as efficiently as it will cut wood.) If the reasoner starts from well-established premises, he will reach conclusions in which he may have confidence. If he starts from premises which are false, reason will take him into ' error's fenny bogs and thorny brakes.' Moral : make sure by experiment and observation that your premises are correct.

Where life in general is concerned, it is impossible to have adequate data. All that the individual reasoner has by way of data is his own individual experience and his own feeling about that experience. (Incidentally, he may, in the course of his life, have many and contradictory feelings about his experience ; but we will suppose, for the sake of argument, that one feeling predominates.) The feeling he has about his own experience is the reasoner's major premiss. Or rather, since it is impossible to base an argument on a feeling, it is the rationalization of that feeling in terms of a concept which serves as the major premiss.

We rationalize our feelings easily, almost automatically. The process is so natural to us, that we seldom realize how unjustifiably we resort to it. If I wake up on a fine summer morning, feeling exceptionally well and high spirited, it does not follow that God's in his heaven and all's right with the world. But it is precisely on such rationalizations of feelings that theologies are founded, and it is from such rationalizations that reason leads men, by inexorable logic, into those quagmires of error, over those mountains of whimsies, which Rochester has described. Whitman gives us, in the raw, so to speak, his feeling about experience—a feeling which might easily be rationalized into the major premiss of a theology. Rendered thus, the emotion seems vague enough, in all conscience. But, however vague, it is all we are given. The elaborate constructions of theology are based, as Otto has insisted, on the rationalizations of just such dim and hardly describable ' numinous ' feelings. Any system of clear-cut concepts based upon data so obscure and inadequate can hardly fail to be incorrect.

If we would avoid the fenny bogs and thorny brakes, we must imitate the self-denying Whitman and refrain from arbitrary rationalizations and headlong rushes to logical conclusions. Or if we must play the theological game, let us never forget that it is a game. Religion, it seems to me, can survive only as a consciously accepted system of make-believe. People will accept certain theological statements about life and the world, will elect to perform certain rites and to follow certain rules of conduct, not because they imagine the statements to be true or the rules and rites to be divinely dictated, but simply because they have discovered experimentally that to live in a certain ritual rhythm, under certain ethical restraints, and as if certain metaphysical doctrines were true, is to live nobly, with style. Every art has its conventions which every artist must accept. The greatest, the most important of the arts is living.

# INDEX

## OF AUTHORS QUOTED